# Pillow Party!

## Creating Pillows from Quilt Blocks

### Pamela Lindquist

*Martingale*®
& COMPANY

# Credits

CEO: Daniel J. Martin
President: Nancy J. Martin
Publisher: Jane Hamada
Editorial Director: Mary V. Green
Managing Editor: Tina Cook
Technical Editor: Barbara Weiland
Copy Editor: Liz McGehee
Design Director: Stan Green
Illustrator: Robin Strobel
Cover and Text Designer: Regina Girard
Photographer: Brent Kane

That Patchwork Place® is an imprint
of Martingale & Company®.

Pillow Party!: Creating Pillows from Quilt Blocks
© 2004 by Pamela Lindquist

Martingale & Company
20205 144th Avenue NE
Woodinville, WA 98072-8478 USA
www.martingale-pub.com

Printed in China
09 08 07 06 05 04          8 7 6 5 4 3 2 1

## Mission Statement

Dedicated to providing quality products
and service to inspire creativity.

**Library of Congress Cataloging-in-Publication Data**
Lindquist, Pamela.
   Pillow party! : creating pillows from quilt blocks /
Pamela Lindquist.
      p.  cm.
   Includes bibliographical references.
   ISBN 1-56477-563-1
   1. Patchwork—Patterns.  2. Quilting.  3. Pillows.
I. Title.
   TT835 .L63697  2004
   746 .46 ' 0437—dc22

                                    2004003594

# Dedication

*To the many quilt guilds around the world. Quilt guilds exist to share information on quilting, encourage learning, participate in community service, and provide camaraderie and fellowship for like-minded enthusiasts. They challenge and inspire us in our quilting endeavors.*

*A small group of women, some of whom recently participated in one of the author's pillow workshops, gathers before the monthly meeting of the Emerald Valley Quilt Guild in Eugene, Oregon. With almost three hundred members, the guild provides many opportunities to educate, share, and serve.*

# Acknowledgments

My sincere thanks to:

Benartex Incorporated for their very generous support in providing many of the wonderful fabrics used in this book;

Professional quilter Sheila Snyder for her beautiful machine quilting on many of the pillows in this book;

June and John Macauley of QuiltMasters, who used their computerized custom-quilting system to turn yards of wonderful fabrics into stunning whole-cloth quilts;

The staff at Martingale & Company for providing incredible technical support that helped me put my ideas into book form;

My quilting buddies in the Emerald Valley Quilt Guild, who have been very supportive with their kind words and interest in my projects;

My husband, Rick, and my children, Nathan and Sarah, who have held the home front together while I have been "stitching."

# Contents

Introduction                                          6

Planning Your Pillow                                  7

Pillow-Making Basics                                  8

Square and Rectangular Pillows                       18
*Whole-Cloth Trapunto Pillow*                        19
*Tudor Rose Appliquéd Pillow*                        22
*Fuchsia-in-the-Summer-
    Wind Pillow*                                     26
*Flowers-in-a-Row Pillow*                            29

Shaped Pillows                                        32
*Ruffled Round Pillow*                               34
*Striped Wedge Pillow*                               36
*Scrappy Flower Wedge Pillow*                        38
*Floral Wreath Pillow*                               40
*Leafy Heart Pillow*                                 43
*Ruffled Heart Pillow*                               47

Neckrolls                                            49
*Garden Lattice Neckroll*                            50
*Stars All Around Neckroll*                          53
*Ruffled Drawstring Neckroll*                        56

**Pillow Shams and Pillowcases**  59

 *Whole-Cloth Trapunto Pillow Shams* 60

 *Blueberry Vine Pillow Shams* 64

 *Whole-Cloth Rose Medallion Trapunto*
  *Pillow Shams* 66

 *Appliquéd Rose Pillow Shams* 71

 *Pieced European Pillow Shams* 75

 *Decorative Pillowcases* 78

**Bibliography**  80

**About the Author**  80

# Introduction

Pillows are wonderful, decorative accents in almost any room setting. They pack a lot of punch for their size, adding visual impact and a splash of color. In addition to choosing from a variety of sizes and shapes, you can combine fabrics and trims to create pillows that reflect your decorating style while adding color and comfort to the room. Making a pillow requires only a small investment in time and materials, and the results can vary from simple to elaborate, casual to formal, or delicate to durable.

When you use quiltmaking skills to make your own decorative pillows, you expand the creative opportunities to experiment with fabric, color, and design. Team classic quilt patterns with today's wonderful fabrics and quick-sew techniques, and you have the makings of pretty and practical decor for your home.

# Planning Your Pillow

This book includes directions for making a variety of pillows and pillow coverings (shams and pillowcases). The pillows include three basic styles, each with its own particular decorative appeal and/or practical value.

*Rectangular and Square Pillows:* Straight seams define these shapes. They can be made with knife edges or with boxed edges (see box below).

*Shaped Pillows:* Curved seaming creates shapely pillows. Shaped pillows can be made with knife edges or with boxed edges.

*Neckrolls:* These are small, cylindrical pillows similar to bolsters.

When deciding on the appropriate combination of materials and design elements for your pillow project, it is important to think about the room setting and your design goals. Let the following questions guide you in blending pillow design and function to create the perfect pillow.

- Is this pillow mainly for decor or function?

- Which style, shape, and size of pillow would best meet my decorating goal?

- What mood or look do I want to create—simple or elaborate, casual or formal, delicate or durable?

- How often will the pillow need to be laundered? Will it require an easy-on-and-off closure?

- Which types of trims are appropriate?

- Which fabrics and colors do I want to use? If the pillow fabric is printed, does the scale of the motifs work well with the desired pillow shape and size?

Using basic sewing skills and the directions in this book, you can create unique, custom-sewn pillows and pillow covers that coordinate with your decor. The patterns and the simple step-by-step directions focus on a variety of techniques, including piecework, appliqué, quilting, embroidery, and embellishment. Have fun planning and finishing your pillow projects.

*Pam Lindquist*

---

Knife-edge pillows are the simplest pillows to make. Two pieces of fabric are simply sewn together, turned right side out, and stuffed. Edges may be plain, corded, or ruffled.

Box-edge pillows require two pieces of fabric cut to the same shape, plus a boxing strip cut to match the thickness of the pillow form, plus seam allowances. The added strip gives the pillow more "cushion." The seams can be plain or corded.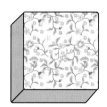

# Pillow-Making Basics

Refer to this section of the book often as you follow the directions for the pillow project you have chosen. It includes a variety of basic sewing techniques and information about pillows that you should understand before you begin.

## Fabric, Filler, and Embellishments

Every pillow has an outer cover and a filler. The cover, like those in this book, is often made with a decorative top and a plain back. Some pillow-cover tops have additional decorative embellishments.

Today's high-quality, printed quilting cottons are a wonderful choice for home decor. With so many beautifully coordinated fabric collections available, it's easy to choose fabrics in colors and styles that complement each other. Florals, stripes, and plaids can look great together in a patchwork pillow when the colors are carefully chosen. Although quilting fabrics are lighter weight than many decorating fabrics, pillows made with them can still be quite durable. The added layers in the front of the quilted pillow cover, plus any special edge treatments, add to their durability.

**Note:** Before beginning your pillow, it's a good idea to prewash the fabrics, using the same laundering method you will use for the finished pillow. It is usually unnecessary to prewash batting, but check the directions on the packaging to make sure.

The pillows in this book get their shape from ready-made polyester pillow forms or from custom-made inserts stuffed with polyester fiberfill. Polyester fiberfill and pillow forms are inexpensive, washable, nonallergenic, and resilient—a truly compatible choice for pillows made from quilting fabrics.

Pillow forms in standard sizes (12", 14", and 16" squares are the most common) are readily available at fabric and quilt shops. You can also have box-edge foam pillows cut to size in some home-decorating departments. Or, you can make your own inserts by sewing a muslin cover in the shape and size of the pillow you are making and then stuffing it with loose polyester fiberfill to the desired firmness. Using a ready-made insert (or one you make yourself) is recommended, particularly if you plan to launder or dry-clean the pillow cover periodically.

*Pillow Forms*

Braid, lace, ribbon, piping, buttons, and beads—the list of possible embellishments for your pillow is a long one. Consider making your own embellishments using coordinating quilting fabrics for ruffles, cording, appliqués, and covered buttons. Hand or machine embroidery and fabric painting are other embellishment techniques to consider. As you choose embellishments, consider how and where the pillow will be used and how often it will need to be laundered.

# Basic Sewing Tools

Besides a well-maintained sewing machine, you need only a few basic sewing tools to get started making wonderful quilted pillows.

*Pencil, chalk, and nonpermanent ink markers.* What you choose for marking depends on the fabric color and type and what you need to mark. Pretest any of these methods on a fabric scrap before using it on the pillow top. Pressing over marks may heat-set them, so take care in this regard.

*Rotary cutter, ruler, and mat.* Rotary cutting and strip piecing save time and increase accuracy. Choose a large mat and a 24"-long ruler for best results.

*Sewing-machine presser feet.* In addition to the all-purpose presser foot, three other presser feet are very useful for pillow construction. Choose a walking foot (or the built-in, even-feed feature if your machine has it) to feed the thick layers of a pillow through your machine. You may also want to use it for quilting the layers together in the completed pillow top. A darning foot is useful for free-motion machine quilting. A zipper foot is essential for inserting zippers in removable covers, but it also helps when applying hook-and-loop tape and snap closures, as well as sewing cording or other decorative trims to your pillow.

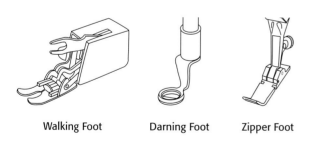

Walking Foot          Darning Foot          Zipper Foot

*Sharp shears and small embroidery scissors.* Use these tools to clip curves accurately and trim away excess fabric thickness or loose threads.

*Standard steam/dry iron.* Careful pressing is essential with all patchwork techniques.

*Tape measure.* Use to measure pillow forms as well as to cut trim to the appropriate length.

# Pillow-Construction Glossary

Familiarize yourself with the following construction terms before you begin your pillow project.

**Baste:** Use long, easy-to-remove stitches to sew the fabric layers together temporarily, either by hand or by machine.

**Bias strips:** These are fabric strips cut on the bias or diagonal of the fabric. The give in bias makes bias strips behave when applying cording to the edges of pillow covers or when using them to make appliqué pieces.

**Mark:** Draw temporary guidelines on a piece of fabric. Use a pencil, dressmaker's chalk, or a non-permanent-ink marking pen. Test for removability on your fabric.

**Seam allowances:** When piecing quilt blocks, use a ¼"-wide seam allowance to keep bulk to a minimum. For the actual pillow construction, however, use a ½"-wide seam allowance, which is the standard for most home-decorating projects. The wider seam allowance helps reinforce outer-edge seams, which are under the most stress in a completed pillow.

**Slip-stitch:** Use a hand-sewing needle and thread to sew two seams together invisibly. This is the recommended method for finishing an opening left in a seam of a pillow cover so you can turn it right side out and insert the pillow form or stuffing. This is not the recommended closure if you wish to launder the pillow cover, since it requires opening the seam to remove the pillow insert and then restitching it after laundering.

**Topstitch:** Stitch through multiple layers at a specified width (most often ¼" from a seam line) for a decorative accent and/or to hold seam allowances in place.

# Cutting Bias Strips

Bias strips are often used to make covered cording or piping. To cut bias strips of the appropriate width and length (as given in individual pillow-project directions):

1. Begin with a straight-grain square of fabric. The project instructions will tell you what size square to cut. Using a rotary cutter and ruler, make a diagonal cut from one corner to the opposite corner.

2. Measure the desired width of the bias strip from the first diagonal cut and cut again. Continue measuring and cutting strips from the fabric in this manner until you have enough strips to make the length required for your project.

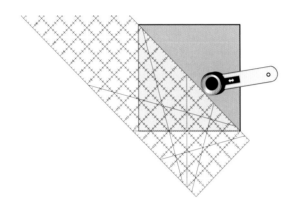

Cut diagonally from corner to corner.

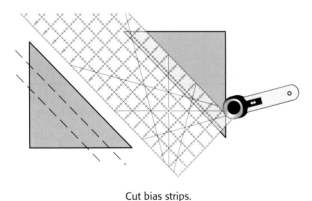

Cut bias strips.

3. Sew the strips together with diagonal seams, press the seams open, and trim.

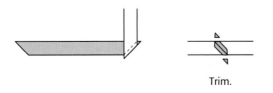

Trim.

# Making Bias Vines for Appliqué

To make bias stems and vines, use bias strips.

1. Cut the bias strips as directed at left. The project instructions will tell you what width to cut the strips. Sew together as needed to make pieces of the required lengths.

2. To create a bias tube, fold the strip in half lengthwise with wrong sides together and raw edges even. Stitch ¼" from the raw edges. For narrow stems or vines, trim the seam allowance to ⅛". Position the seam in the center of the tube and press the seam allowance to one side.

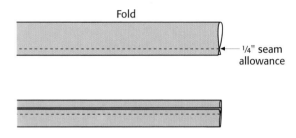

Fold

¼" seam allowance

# Making Half-Square-Triangle Units

You will need these units for some of the patchwork pillow tops in this book. Following are my favorite methods for making accurate units. I use the first method when I am making only a few units and the second when I need a large quantity. I also suggest using the Bias Square® ruler developed by Nancy J. Martin and distributed by Martingale & Company. It is a very useful tool for "squaring up" or trimming the units.

## Method One

With this method, you will pair squares of two different fabrics together. You will get two units from each pair of squares.

1. Cut the squares 1" larger than the desired finished size of the half-square-triangle unit.

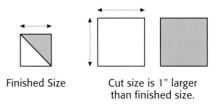

Finished Size

Cut size is 1" larger than finished size.

2. Layer the squares, right sides together, with the lighter color on top of the darker color.

3. Use a pencil and ruler to draw a diagonal line from corner to corner on the wrong side of the lighter fabric.

4. Stitch ¼" away from the drawn line on each side. Cut on the pencil line.

5. Open each resulting triangle unit and press toward the darker triangle in each unit. Use the 8" Bias Square to trim the unit to the desired unfinished size (as specified in the patchwork directions).

## Method Two

With this method, you begin with identically sized squares or rectangles of two different fabrics. Refer to the directions for the pillow project you are making for the size to cut.

1. Place the two fabric squares or rectangles right sides together, with raw edges even.

2. Using a rotary cutter and ruler, make a diagonal cut from one corner to the opposite one.

3. Cut bias strips of the desired width (as indicated in your project directions) from the layered pieces. Cut the strips ½" wider than the desired unfinished size for the unit. For example, to make 1½" half-square-triangle units that will finish to 1" square in the patchwork, you would cut the bias

strips 2" wide. Cut the required number of strips for the project you are making.

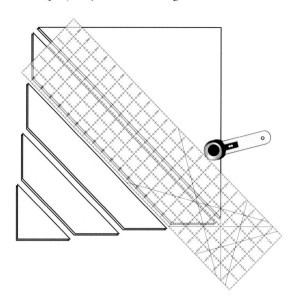

4. Using ¼"-wide seam allowances, sew the fabric strips together on the long bias edge of each pair. Press the seams open. Sew the strip pairs together as shown, sewing the longest strip pairs together, then the next longest, and so on, until all the strips are connected. Use a rotary cutter and the 8" Bias Square ruler to cut half-square-triangle units from the piece.

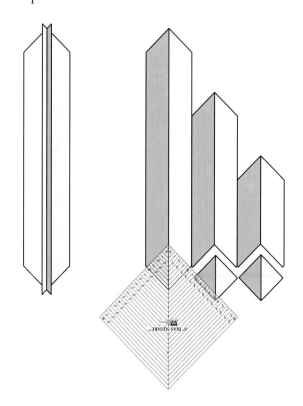

# Quilting a Pillow Top

Besides the practical aspect of holding the pillow top, batting, and backing layers together, hand or machine quilting adds visual texture and eye appeal to the completed pillow top. Thoughtful consideration of quilting options and patterns should be integrated into the overall pillow design. Stitch-in-the-ditch, echo, meandering, and cross-hatch quilting are all possibilities to consider.

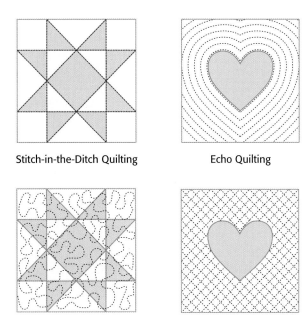

Stitch-in-the-Ditch Quilting     Echo Quilting

Meander Quilting     Cross-Hatch Quilting

In addition to hand and machine quilting, this book includes trapunto quilting. Trapunto gives the pillow top a padded or sculpted effect. It is usually most successful when used on whole-cloth projects. Machine trapunto is a modern method that is easy to learn and gives great results.

## Machine or Hand Quilting

Choose your favorite quilting method to add texture and depth to the pillow top. Prepare for quilting by following the steps below.

1. Cut the batting and backing 2" larger all around than the finished pillow top.

2. Layer the pillow top with batting and backing (use muslin or scrap fabric). Baste the layers together.

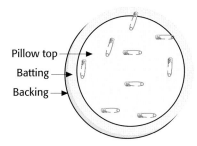

Pillow top
Batting
Backing

3. Quilt as desired.

4. Stitch ⅛" from the pillow-top raw edges through all layers. Trim the excess batting and backing even with the pillow top.

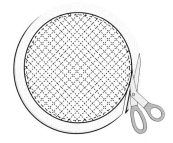

Stitch ⅛" from raw edge of pillow top.
Trim excess batting and backing.

## Machine Trapunto

Follow the easy steps below to create the elegant textural effect of trapunto. You will need high-loft quilt batting, low-loft batting, and water-soluble thread to achieve the desired results.

1. Use your favorite nonpermanent marking method to trace the desired quilting design onto the right side of the pillow top.

2. Layer the marked pillow top, right side up, on top of a piece of high-loft batting that is 1" larger all around than the pillow top. Pin in place.

Pin in place.

3. With regular thread in the bobbin and water-soluble basting thread in the sewing-machine needle, stitch just inside the lines of the marked design (¹⁄₁₆" inside the lines).

Stitch inside the traced lines with water-soluble thread.

4. Turn the pillow top over and trim away the batting between the outline-stitched design motifs. Use a blunt-tipped scissors and trim as close as possible to the quilting-motif outline stitches. Take care not to cut the pillow top.

5. Layer the prepared pillow top with a piece of low-loft batting and backing. Baste the layers together.

6. With regular quilting thread in the sewing-machine needle, stitch on the marked lines for the quilting motif.

7. Quilt in the background or open areas outside the design with a closely stitched, meandering design.

Layer scrap backing, batting, and pillow top, and quilt closely in non-trapunto areas.

8. To remove water-soluble thread, immerse your pillow top in clear, tepid water. Let it soak for one to two minutes and swish it around by hand for a few seconds. The water-soluble thread will dissolve, and if you used a water-soluble-ink marker the lines will disappear.

# Choosing Decorative Elements for Pillows

Your choice of trimmings and edge treatments defines the pillow's style. Decorative trims are often topstitched to the surface of the pillow. Choices include woven braid, lace, ribbon, and cord, to mention a few. Mail-order catalogs, home-decorating magazines, and the home-decorating departments of your favorite stores are great places to look for pillow-trimming ideas.

One of the bonuses of sewing your own pillows is that you can make your own edge treatments using quilting fabrics that coordinate beautifully with the other fabrics in your pillow. Cording and ruffles are the two most common edge treatments for pillows. Used alone or in combination, in matching or contrasting colors, edge treatments can give a single pillow style an endless number of finished looks. You can purchase ready-made cording or make your own. You may be able to purchase ready-made ruffled trims for your pillows, but chances are, you will need to make your own ruffles. Directions for making covered cording and gathered ruffles using matching or coordinating fabrics are included below.

Adding a border to a decorative pillow top is another wonderful finishing touch. Use either straight-cut or mitered corners on the border as you prefer.

A straight-cut border is the easiest to cut and attach. However, if you wish to insert trim or lace in the seams between the border and the center panel, choose a mitered border as the pillow-top "frame."

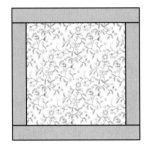 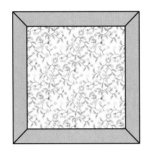

Straight-Cut Border          Mitered Border

Other decorative options include adding prairie points at the edge or adding a flange (a "flat" ruffle) that extends beyond the pillow edge.

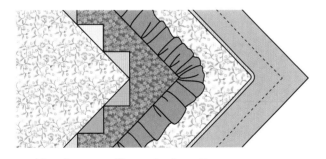

Prairie Points    Ruffle    Cording    Flange

## Covered Cording

Cording is decorative but also functional since it makes the pillow edges more durable and protects seams from undue wear. Covered cording usually has a cotton-cord filler and is often referred to as welting or piping. The fabric covering may be cut on the straight grain or the bias. Many sewing reference sources recommend bias strips to make it easier to turn corners with the finished

cording. However, while doing upholstery work, I experimented with straight-grain strips (the standard in the upholstery industry). I discovered they are easier to work with than bias strips when using the lighter-weight quilting fabrics and that there is little difference in the finished appearance. For that reason, the yardage and directions in this book are based on cutting straight-grain strips. Of course, you are free to cut bias strips if you prefer, but you will need additional yardage. In some cases, bias covering for the cord may be desirable. For example, cutting a stripe or plaid on the bias adds a nice design element.

*To make covered cording:*

1. Cut strips of the width required as directed for the pillow you are making.

2. Join the strips using bias seams as shown to avoid lumps in the finished cord.

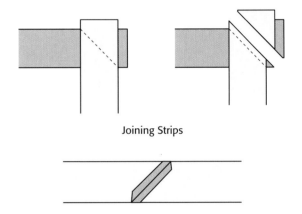

Joining Strips

3. Center the filler cord on the wrong side of the strip and wrap the fabric around it with raw edges even.

4. Using a zipper foot, machine baste along the cord to enclose it in the fabric strip.

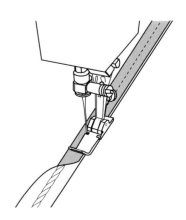

*To attach covered cording:*

1. Beginning at the midpoint along one edge of the pillow top, position the covered cording on the right side with the raw edges even.

2. Using the zipper foot and a ½"-wide seam allowance, machine baste the cording in place. Begin stitching 1½" from one end of the covered cording.

3. When you reach a corner, stop stitching and clip the cording seam allowance to the basting stitches to allow it to flex and turn the corner. To turn the corner, stitch to within ½" of the pillow-top corner. Sink the needle into the fabric, raise the presser foot, and then pivot the fabric and the cording. Lower the presser foot and continue stitching along the remainder of the pillow to within 1½" of the beginning of the cording. Sink the needle into the fabric and cut away any excess cording, leaving 1" extra.

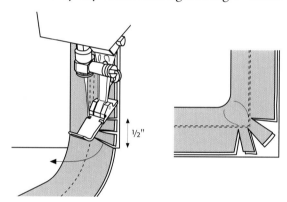

4. Push the covering down along the end of the cording so you can trim the cord inside; it will then butt up against the cord at the beginning end. Turn under ½" at the trimmed end of the covered cording and slip the other end inside as shown. Complete the stitching.

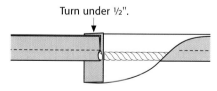

To join cording, trim cord so ends abut.

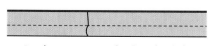

Overlap to cover ends of cord. Stitch.

## Ruffles

A double-layer, gathered ruffle adds a soft touch to the outer edge of a finished pillow. You will need to gather long expanses of fabric to fit the outer edge of the completed pillow top.

1. Cut the ruffle strips as directed for the pillow you are making.

2. Sew the ruffle strips together, end to end, to create one large circle of fabric. Press the seams open.

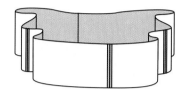

3. Fold the ruffle in half with wrong sides together and raw edges even; press.

4. Adjust the machine for a basting-length stitch (4mm or longer).

5. Draw up the bobbin threads to gather the ruffle so it fits the outer edge of the pillow top. Adjust the gathers evenly and pin to the pillow top before stitching in place a scant ½" from the raw edges.

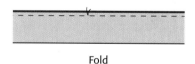

Fold

# Pillow Closures and Fastenings

If you wish to launder your pillow cover, it must have an opening in back so that you can remove the insert. The fastening you choose can be decorative or functional. The pillows in this book have a classic lapped envelope closure and the pieces for the back are cut to allow for this. If you prefer, you can substitute a zipper closure by following the sewing and trimming directions that follow.

## Making an Overlapped Envelope Closure

This is one of the easiest methods for making a removable pillow cover. It is also the classic closure for the back of a pillow sham.

1. Turn under and press a 1"-wide hem on both backing pieces. Turn under again and press. Stitch close to the inner folded edge. *Optional:* Add hook-and-loop tape, snap tape, or buttons and buttonholes now.

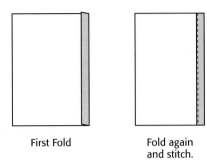

First Fold        Fold again
and stitch.

2. With right sides together and raw edges even, position one of the hemmed pieces on the completed pillow top. Place the remaining piece on top and pin the layers together.

3. Stitch the backing to the pillow top or sham ½" from the raw edges.

4. Turn the pillow cover or sham right side out and insert the pillow form or pillow.

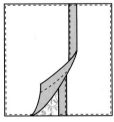 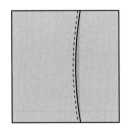

Stitch backing to the top.    Turn right side out.

**Note:** If you want a more secure envelope closure, especially if you are using a firm, plump pillow form, add a hook-and-loop or snap tape fastener to the finished edges of the opening.

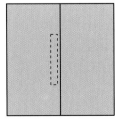

Hook-and-Loop or
Snap Tape Fastener

## Substituting a Zipped Pillow Closure

After cutting the pieces for the pillow back as directed for the pillow you are making, follow these steps to insert a zipper. For a 14"-square pillow, you will need a 12"-long zipper. For other pillow shapes and sizes, use a zipper that is approximately 2" shorter than the opening and adapt the following directions as needed. You will also need a zipper foot for your machine.

1. Layer the two back panels with right sides together. Using a ¾" seam allowance, stitch for 1½" and then backstitch. Do not clip the thread. Change to a basting-length stitch and stitch the next 12". Backstitch. Change to the normal stitch length and complete the seam. Press the seam open.

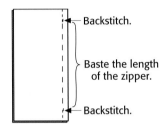

Backstitch.

Baste the length
of the zipper.

Backstitch.

2. Attach the zipper foot, moving it to the right of the needle. Unzip the zipper. With the zipper face down and the top and bottom stops at the beginning and end of the basting in the seam, position the zipper on the seam allowance as shown, placing the coil next to the stitching line. Stitch in place along the woven guideline. You will be stitching through the zipper tape and seam allowance only.

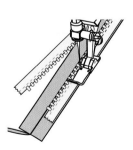

3. Zip the zipper and turn it face up, forming a fold in the seam allowance. Move the zipper foot to the left of the needle and stitch close to the fold through all layers.

4. Stitching through the pillow back and seam allowance, baste the remaining half of the zipper along the woven guideline and across both ends. Move the zipper foot to the right of the needle and stitch the zipper in place from the right side. Remove the basting.

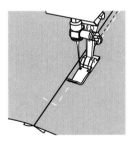

5. Center the pillow top on the zipped back and trim the back to match. *Unzip* the zipper. Pin and stitch the front and back together ½" from the raw edges. Turn the pillow cover right side out through the zipper opening and insert the pillow form.

Lapped Zipper

# Additional Ideas for Pillow Closures

Buttons and loops or buttons and buttonholes are functional closures but can be decorative, depending on your choice of buttons.

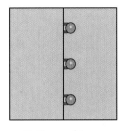

Button-and-Loop Closure

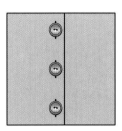

Buttons and Buttonholes

Ties are another decorative option for holding a pillow insert in place.

Ties

Decorative drawstrings are often used at the ends of neckrolls.

Drawstring

# Square and Rectangular Pillows

*This pillow style is the most versatile and the easiest to construct. Choose from pieced, appliquéd, and trapunto-quilted pillow projects in this section. Feel free to use the basic directions and dimensions for any of these designs as a springboard for substituting other pieced and appliquéd designs to complement your decor.*

# Whole-Cloth Trapunto Pillow

**Finished Size:** 16" x 16"

*Machine trapunto adds lovely depth and texture to the quilted design on this simple pillow edged with fabric-covered cording.*

## Materials

*Yardage is based on 42"-wide fabric.*

1¼ yards of blue tone-on-tone print for pillow top and back and covered cording

18" x 18" square of high-loft polyester batting for trapunto

18" x 18" square of scrap backing

18" x 18" square of batting

2⅛ yards of ½"-diameter cotton cording for covered cording

Water-soluble basting thread

16" x 16" knife-edge pillow insert

## Cutting

*All measurements include ½"-wide seam allowances.*

**From the blue tone-on-tone print, cut:**

- 1 square, 17" x 17"
- 1 strip, 13" x 42"; crosscut 2 pieces, 13" x 17"
- 2 strips, 2¾" x 42"

## Pillow-Top Assembly

1. Use your favorite nonpermanent marking method to draw a 16" x 16" square on the right side in the center of the 17" square of blue tone-on-tone print.

2. Referring to the illustration below for placement, enlarge the trapunto design on page 21 and draw it inside the marked lines on the pillow top.

Fold fabric in half lengthwise and crosswise to find the center.

3. Place the marked pillow top, right side up, on the 18" square of high-loft batting. Pin in place.

4. Following the directions on page 12, complete the machine trapunto and quilting on the pillow top.

5. Stitch ⅛" from the outer raw edges of the completed pillow top, sewing through all layers. Trim the excess batting and backing even with the pillow-top edges.

6. Remove the water-soluble thread and markings as directed in step 8 on page 13.

7. Sew the 2¾" x 42" strips together and press the seam open. Use the strip to make covered cording as directed on page 14. Baste the covered cording to the pillow top, following the directions on page 15.

## Pillow Finishing

1. Sew a 1"-wide double-fold hem on a 17"-long edge of each of the 13" x 17" pillow-back pieces as directed on page 16.

2. With right sides together and raw edges even, position one hemmed piece on the quilted pillow top. Add the remaining backing piece and pin the layers together. Stitch ½" from the raw edge.

3. Turn the completed pillow cover right side out and insert the pillow form.

**Whole-Cloth Trapunto Pillow**
Enlarge pattern 225%.

# Tudor Rose Appliquéd Pillow

**Finished Size:** 16" x 16"

*Use the same design elements as those shown for the whole-cloth trapunto pillow shown on page 19 with your favorite appliqué method (hand, machine, or fusible) to create a lovely appliquéd pillow. Tone-on-tone prints were used for the pillow shown, but you may substitute other prints or solids to coordinate with your decorating scheme.*

## Materials

*Yardage is based on 42"-wide fabric.*

1⅛ yards of light blue fabric for pillow top and back

⅜ yard of dark green fabric for leaf appliqués and covered cording on outer edge

⅜ yard of medium green fabric for leaf appliqués and covered cording around center appliqué

11" x 11" piece of dark blue solid or tone-on-tone print for center appliqué

10" x 10" piece of medium blue tone-on-tone print for center appliqué

8" x 8" piece of gold tone-on-tone print for center appliqué

4" x 4" scraps of a light and a medium blue print or solid for center appliqué circles

18" x 18" square of scrap backing

18" x 18" square of batting

2⅛ yards of ¼"-diameter cording for covered cording on outer edge

1⅛ yards of ⅛"-diameter cording for covered cording around center appliqué

16" x 16" knife-edge pillow form

*Optional:* Beads to embellish appliqués

## Cutting

*All measurements include ½"-wide seam allowances.*

**From the light blue fabric, cut:**
- 1 square, 17" x 17"
- 1 strip, 13" x 42"; crosscut 2 pieces, 13" x 17"

**From the medium green fabric, cut:**
- 1 strip, 1½" x 42"

**From the dark green fabric, cut:**
- 2 strips, 2" x 42"

# Pillow-Top Assembly

1. Choose your favorite appliqué method: hand, machine, or fusible. Make templates for the appliqué shapes using the patterns on pages 24–25. If you will be turning under the edges of your appliqué shapes, add a scant ¼" turn-under allowance beyond the edges of the shapes as you cut them out.

2. Cut the required number of each appliqué shape from the appropriate fabrics as indicated on the pattern pieces.

3. Using the 1½" x 42" medium green strip and the ⅛"-diameter cording, make covered cording as directed on page 14.

4. Use your favorite nonpermanent marking method to draw a 16" x 16" square in the center of the 17" square of light blue fabric. Referring to the illustration below, trace the large center motif in the center of the square as a placement guide for the medium green covered cording. Mark the positions for the remaining appliqué shapes.

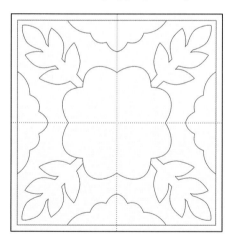

Mark the positions of the appliqué shapes.

5. Position appliqués 1 and 2 over the markings and sew or fuse in place.

6. Position and baste the medium green covered cording along the marking for the large flower appliqué in the center. Position so the cording seam allowance extends toward the center of the

shape and the basting in the covered cording follows the marked line.

Baste cording, stitching on the marked line.

7. Position and sew the remaining appliqués in place in numerical order to complete the floral center.

8. *Optional:* Embellish the appliqués with decorative beads if desired.

9. Layer the appliquéd square with the 18" squares of batting and backing. Baste the layers together and quilt as desired.

10. Stitch ⅛" from the outer raw edges of the appliquéd pillow top, sewing through all layers. Trim the excess batting and backing even with the pillow-top edges.

11. Sew the dark green 2" x 42" strips together and press the seams open. Make covered cording using the strip and the ¼"-diameter cording as directed on page 14.

12. Position and baste the covered cording in place along the outer edge of the pillow top, joining the ends as directed on page 15.

# Pillow Finishing

1. Sew a 1"-wide double-fold hem on a 17"-long edge of each 13" x 17" pillow-back piece as directed on page 16.

2. With right sides together and raw edges even, position one of the hemmed pieces on the quilted pillow top. Add the remaining hemmed piece and pin the layers together. Stitch ½" from the raw edges.

3. Turn the completed pillow cover right side out and insert the pillow form.

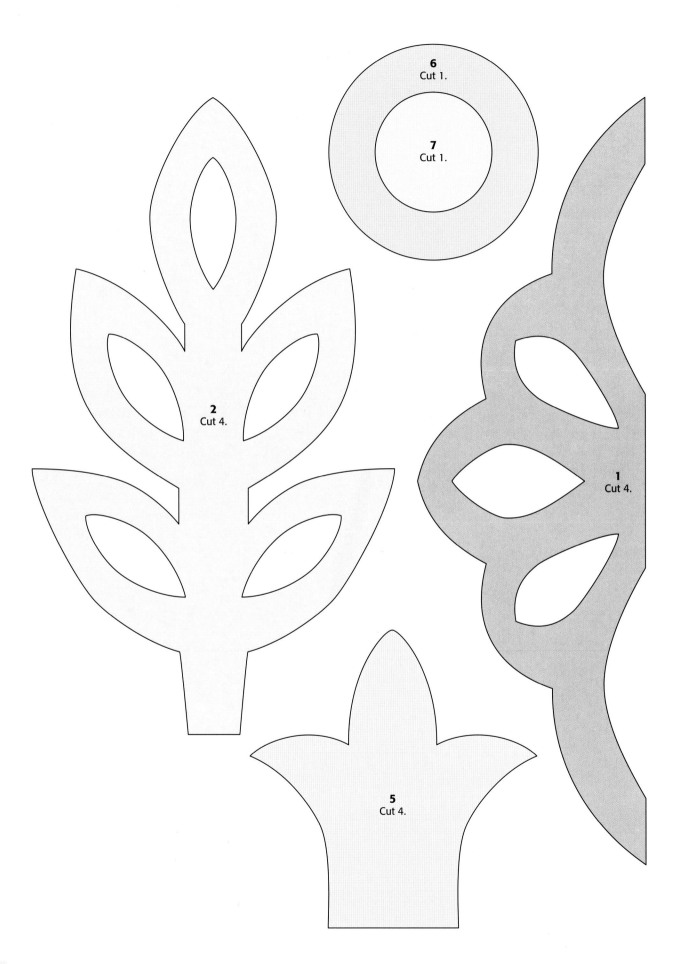

**6**
Cut 1.

**7**
Cut 1.

**2**
Cut 4.

**1**
Cut 4.

**5**
Cut 4.

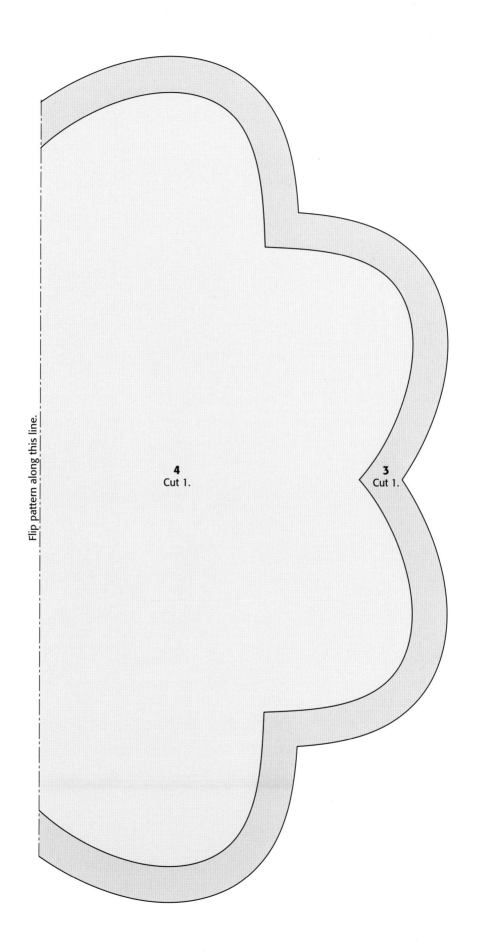

Flip pattern along this line.

**4**
Cut 1.

**3**
Cut 1.

# Fuchsia-in-the-Summer-Wind Pillow

**Finished Size:** 16" x 16"

*It's easy to turn any 12"-square quilt block into a wonderful 16"-square pillow by adding 2"-wide borders all around. Try this simple pieced block for the pillow top as shown or as the backdrop for an appliquéd floral wreath.*

## Materials

*Yardage is based on 42"-wide fabric.*

¾ yard of purple print for borders and pillow back

⅜ yard of tone-on-tone print for block

¼ yard of lavender print for block

*Optional:* Scraps of purple, pink, and green for appliqués

18" x 18" square of scrap backing

18" x 18" square of batting

*Optional:* Dark green and gold embroidery floss for embroidered details on appliqués

16" x 16" knife-edge pillow form

*Optional:* Beads to embellish appliqués

## Cutting

*All measurements include ¼"-wide seam allowances.*

**From the lavender print, cut:**
- 1 strip, 3" x 42"
- 1 strip, 2½" x 42"; crosscut:
    4 squares, 2½" x 2½"
    4 rectangles, 2½" x 4½"

**From the tone-on-tone print, cut:**
- 1 strip, 3" x 42"
- 1 strip, 2½" x 42"; crosscut 8 squares, 2½" x 2½"
- 1 strip, 4½" x 42"; crosscut:
    4 rectangles, 2½" x 4½"
    1 square, 4½" x 4½"

**From the purple print, cut:**

- 1 strip, 13" x 42"; crosscut 2 pieces, 13" x 17"
- 2 strips, 2¾" x 42"; crosscut:
    2 strips, 2¾" x 12½"
    2 strips, 2¾" x 17"

# Pillow-Top Assembly

1. Place the 3"-wide lavender print and tone-on-tone print strips right sides together with raw edges even. From the paired strips, cut six sets of 3" squares. Set the remainder of the strips aside for another project.

2. Following the directions on pages 10–11, make 12 half-square-triangle units from the paired squares. Trim each unit to 2½" square.

3. Using a pencil and ruler, draw a diagonal line from corner to corner on the wrong side of each 2½" tone-on-tone print square.

4. With right sides together, place a marked square face down at one end of a 2½" x 4½" rectangle of lavender print. Stitch on the marked line. Align the ¼" line of a rotary-cutting ruler along the seam line of the square and trim away the excess fabric. Press the seam toward the tone-on-tone print triangle.

   Place a marked square at the other end of the rectangle, right sides together, and stitch along the pencil line. Trim the excess fabric and press the seam toward the tone-on-tone print triangle. Repeat with the remaining squares and rectangles to make a total of four flying-geese units.

Make 4.

5. Arrange the half-square-triangle units, the flying-geese units, and the remaining squares and rectangles in rows, paying careful attention to color placement in the pieced units. Sew the pieces together in rows and press the seams in the direction of the arrows. Sew the rows together to complete the block. Press the seams toward the center row of patchwork.

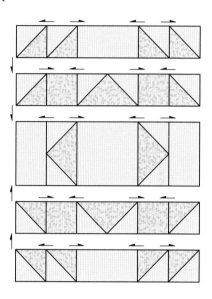

6. Using a ¼"-wide seam allowance, sew the 2¾" x 12½" purple border strips to opposite sides of the pieced pillow top. Press the seam allowances toward the borders. Sew the 2¾" x 17" purple border strips to the top and bottom edges of the pieced pillow top. Press the seam allowances toward the borders.

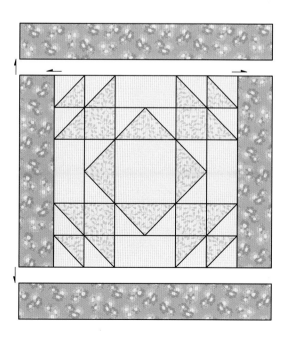

# Optional Appliquéd Wreath

1. Choose your favorite appliqué method: hand, machine, or fusible. Make templates for the leaf and fuchsia appliqué shapes using the patterns below right. If you will be turning under the edges of your appliqué shapes, add a scant ¼" turn-under allowance beyond the edges of the shapes as you cut them out.

2. Cut seven of each appliqué shape from the appropriate fabric scraps as indicated below the pattern pieces.

3. Following the illustration below, position the appliqués and fuse or sew in place. Embroider the stems with a stem stitch and two strands of dark green embroidery floss. Embroider the fuchsia stamens in the same manner, using gold embroidery floss. Make French knots at the ends of the stamens or substitute small beads.

# Pillow Finishing

1. Layer the completed pillow top with the 18" squares of batting and backing. Baste the layers together and quilt as desired.

2. Stitch ⅛" from the outer edge of the pillow top, sewing through all layers. Trim the excess batting and backing even with the pillow-top edges.

3. Sew a 1"-wide double-fold hem on a 17"-long edge of each 13" x 17" pillow-back piece as directed on page 16.

4. With right sides together and raw edges even, position a hemmed pillow-back piece on the quilted pillow top. Add the remaining hemmed piece and pin the layers together. Stitch ½" from the raw edge.

5. Turn the completed pillow cover right side out and insert the pillow form.

Cut 7 of each shape from the appropriate colors.

Stem stitch                    French knot

# Flowers-in-a-Row Pillow

**Finished Size:** 12" x 16"

*Show off your scraps in this colorful garden pillow of easy pieced posies. Prairie points form a playful "fence" around the perimeter of the flower patch.*

## Materials

*Yardage is based on 42"-wide fabric.*

½ yard of dark green print for prairie points

½ yard total of assorted green fabric scraps for leaves and scrappy border

½ yard of medium green print for pillow back

⅜ yard total of assorted red fabric scraps for flowers

⅛ yard total of gold fabric scraps for flower centers

14" x 18" piece of scrap backing

14" x 18" piece of batting

*Optional:* 1⅝ yards of decorative covered cording for outer edge of pillow

12" x 16" pillow insert (see page 8 to make your own)

## Cutting

*All measurements for pieced pillow top include ¼"-wide seam allowances. Measurements for pillow-cover assembly include ½"-wide seam allowances.*

**From the assorted red fabrics, cut:**
- 48 squares, 1½" x 1½" (4 for each flower)
- 24 squares, 2" x 2" (2 for each flower)

**From the assorted green fabrics, cut:**
- 24 squares, 2" x 2" (2 for each flower)
- 18 rectangles, 1½" x 2¾"
- 24 rectangles, 1½" x 2¼"
- 4 rectangles, 2¼" x 2¾"

**From the gold fabrics, cut:**
- 12 squares, 1½" x 1½"

**From the dark green print, cut:**
- 3 strips, 4½" x 42"; crosscut 24 squares, 4½" x 4½"

**From the medium green print, cut:**
- 2 pieces, 13" x 13"

## Flower and Scrappy-Border Assembly

1. Following the directions on pages 10–11, pair each 2" red square with a 2" green square to make half-square-triangle units. Trim each unit to 1½" x 1½". Make four units for each block (48 total).

2. Arrange the half-square-triangle units from step 1 with the 1½" red and the 1½" gold squares in rows to make 12 flower blocks. Sew the pieces together in rows and press the seams in the direction of the arrows. Sew the rows together and press the seams in one direction.

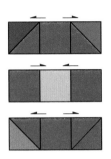 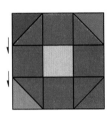

Make 12.

3. Sew the long edges of nine assorted 1½" x 2¾" green rectangles together to make a side border strip that measures 2¾" x 9½". Press all seams in one direction. Repeat with the remaining 1½" x 2¾" green rectangles to make a second border strip.

Make 2.

4. Sew the long edges of 12 assorted 1½" x 2¼" green rectangles together to make a border strip that measures 2¼" x 12½". Press all seams in one direction. Repeat with the remaining 1½" x 2¼" green rectangles to make a second border strip. Sew a 2¼" x 2¾" green rectangle to each end of the 12½"-long pieced strips to make border strips that measure 17" long.

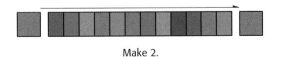

Make 2.

## Pillow-Top Assembly

1. Arrange the flower blocks in three rows of four blocks each. Sew together in rows and press the seams in opposite directions from row to row. Sew the rows together to complete the center of the pillow top. Press the seams in one direction.

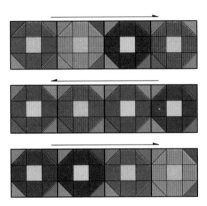

2. Sew the 2¾" x 9½" scrappy green border strips to the short edges of the patchwork and press the seams toward the pillow top. Add the 17"-long top and bottom border strips and press the seams toward the pillow top.

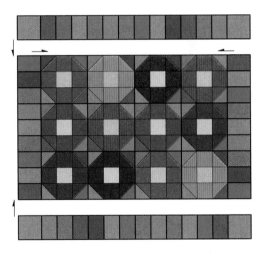

3. Layer the pillow top with the 14" x 18" pieces of batting and backing. Baste the layers together and quilt as desired. Stitch ⅛" from the outer edges of the pillow top, sewing through all layers. Trim the excess batting and backing even with the edges of the pillow top.

4. *Optional:* Machine or hand baste the trim to the outer edge of the pillow top using a ½"-wide seam.

5. Fold each 4½" dark green square in half with wrong sides together and raw edges even. Press. Turn the folded edge down to meet in the center with all raw edges even at the lower edge of the triangle that forms. Press. Make 24 prairie points in this manner.

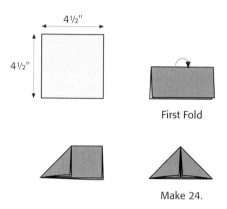

First Fold

Make 24.

6. Arrange the prairie points along the outer edges on the right side of the pillow top, overlapping them as shown. Baste in place.

# Pillow Finishing

1. Sew a 1"-wide double-fold hem on one edge of each of the 13" x 13" pillow-back pieces as directed on page 16.

2. With right sides together and raw edges even, position a hemmed pillow-back piece on the quilted pillow top. Add the remaining hemmed piece and pin the layers together. Stitch ½" from the raw edges.

3. Turn the completed pillow cover right side out and insert the pillow form.

# Designer Tip

*Invite 12 friends to exchange flower blocks. Combine the blocks to make this pillow and you'll have a "friendship bouquet" to enjoy season after season.*

# Shaped Pillows

*Shaped pillows add charm to any decor. This section includes circular and heart-shaped pillow projects. For simplicity's sake, the circular pillows shown in this book are 14" in diameter and the heart-shaped pillows are 16" long. However, you can use the method shown to draft a pattern for a pillow of the desired size. If a ready-made form for the pillow size and shape you design is not available, you can use your pattern to make your own pillow insert as explained on page 8.*

# Making Circle, Wedge, and Heart-Shaped Pillow Patterns

You will need a ruler, protractor, and tissue or tracing paper to make the pattern pieces for shaped pillows.

*To make a pattern for a 14"-diameter pillow:*

1. Fold a 15" x 15" square of tissue paper in half and then in half again.

2. Tie a string to a pencil. Position the pencil tip at one edge of the folded square. Pull the string taut at the corner where the two folded edges meet.

3. Draw an arc from one folded edge of the paper to the other. With the tissue paper still folded, cut along the pencil line.

4. Open the tissue paper to a 15"-diameter circle that includes a ½"-wide seam allowance all around and finishes to a circle with a 14" diameter.

    **Note:** When making patterns for other circle sizes, add 1" to the desired size of the finished circle to cut the tissue square for the pattern.

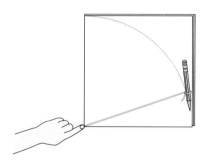

*To make a pattern for an eight-wedge circle pillow:*

1. Make a pattern for a 14" circle as described above.

2. Draw a line through the exact center of the circle (7½" from the outer edge).

3. Position a protractor at the center of the circle and mark the 90° point. Draw a line that bisects the

first line so the circle is divided into quarters. To bisect the quarter wedges, position the protractor and mark the 45° and 135° points. Draw lines across the circle through the center at each of these points to divide the circle into eight equal wedges.

4. Trace one wedge onto a sheet of tissue paper and add ½"-wide seam allowances to the two straight edges only.

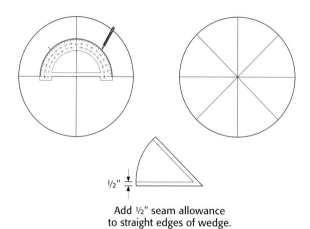

½"

Add ½" seam allowance
to straight edges of wedge.

*To make a 16" heart-shaped pillow pattern:*

1. Fold a 17" x 17" square of tissue paper in half. Beginning at the folded edge, draw half of a heart. With the tissue paper still folded, cut along the pencil line.

2. Open the folded tissue for a heart-shaped pattern that includes ½"-wide seam allowances all around and finishes to 16" long.

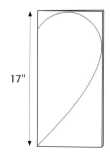
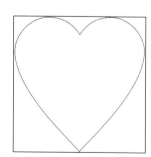

17"

# Ruffled Round Pillow

**Finished Size:** 14" diameter

*Show off a special fabric in a round pillow framed with a contrasting ruffle. Consider using tiny gold or colored beads to embellish the flower centers in the print. Sew them in place through the pillow-top layers to add a quilted effect.*

## Materials

*All yardages are based on 42"-wide fabric.*

⅝ yard of green floral print for pillow top and back

⅝ yard of dark green print or solid for ruffle

¼ yard of red print or solid for covered cording

16" x 16" square of scrap backing

16" x 16" square of batting

1⅝ yards of ⅛"-diameter cotton cording for covered cording

14"-diameter knife-edge pillow form

15" x 15" square of tissue paper for pattern

*Optional:* Beads to embellish flower centers

## Cutting

*All measurements include ½"-wide seam allowances unless otherwise stated.*

**From the green floral print, cut:**
- 1 strip, 15" x 42"; crosscut 2 squares, 15" x 15

**From the dark green fabric, cut:**
- 3 strips, 5" x 42"

**From the red fabric, cut:**
- 2 strips, 1½" x 42"

# Pillow-Cover Assembly

1. Make a tissue-paper pattern for a 14" pillow as directed on page 33.

2. Layer the two 15" green floral squares with raw edges even. Pin the paper pattern to the layers and cut out the circle. Remove the pattern.

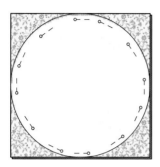

3. Place one of the green floral circles, right side up, on top of the 16" squares of batting and backing. Baste the layers together and quilt as desired. If you wish, embellish the flower centers with beads as described in the photo caption on page 34.

4. Sew the 1½"-wide red strips together and press the seam open. Use the strip to make covered cording and attach it to the pillow top as directed on pages 14–15.

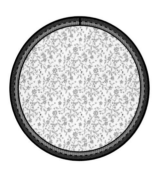

Baste cording to outer edge.

5. Using ¼"-wide seams, sew the dark green 5" x 42" strips together, end to end, to make a circle. Press the seams open. Fold the ruffle in half with wrong sides together and raw edges even; press. Machine baste a scant ½" from the raw edges. Pull on the bobbin thread to gather the ruffle so it fits the outer edge of the pillow top. Pin in place, adjusting the gathers evenly. Baste in place a scant ½" from the raw edge.

6. With right sides together, pin the remaining fabric circle to the pillow top with ruffle. Stitch the layers together, leaving a 5" opening for turning.

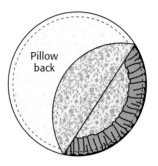

Pillow back

7. Turn the pillow cover right side out and insert the pillow form. Slip-stitch the opening closed.

## Reversible Pillow Tip

Use a dark-fabric pillow back with a light-fabric pillow front to extend your seasonal decorating options. Just flip the pillow over when the seasons change.

# Striped Wedge Pillow

**Finished Size:** 14" diameter

*Cutting wedges from a strip-pieced unit creates a unique ribbon effect on this pillow top. Covered cotton cording criss-crosses the pillow, adding texture and visual interest along the seams and at the outer edge.*

## Materials

*Yardage is based on 42"-wide fabric.*

1 yard of light blue print for pieced wedges, pillow back, and covered cording

¼ yard of medium blue print for pieced wedges

¼ yard of gold print for pieced wedges

16" x 16" square of scrap backing

16" x 16" square of batting

3¾ yards of ⅛"-diameter cotton cording for covered cording

14"-diameter knife-edge pillow form

15" x 15" square of tissue paper for pattern

1"- to 1¼"-diameter decorative button for pillow center

## Cutting

*All measurements include ½"-wide seam allowances unless otherwise noted.*

**From the light blue print, cut:**
- 4 strips, 3" x 42"
- 3 strips, 1½" x 42"
- 1 strip, 15" x 42"; crosscut 1 square, 15" x 15"

**From the medium blue print, cut:**
- 2 strips, 1½" x 42"

**From the gold print, cut:**
- 4 strips, 1" x 42"

## Pillow-Top Assembly

1. Make a tissue-paper pattern for the wedge in an eight-wedge 14"-diameter pillow as directed on page 33.

2. Arrange the 3" light blue strips and the gold and medium blue strips into two strip sets as shown. Sew together with ¼"-wide seams to make two identical strip units. Press all seams away from the center strip in each unit. Center the wedge pattern piece on a strip unit. Pin in place and cut out the wedge. Cut a total of eight identical wedges from the strip units.

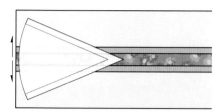

3. Sew the light blue 1½" x 42" strips together and use to cover the ⅛" cording as directed on pages 14–15.

4. Sew cording to the right-hand edge of each of the eight wedges. Set remaining cording aside for the outer edge.

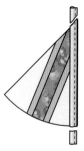

Make 8.

5. With right sides together and using a ½"-wide seam allowance, sew the wedges together in pairs. Use the zipper foot to sew close to the cording. Sew the resulting pairs together to complete the pillow top.

6. Press all seam allowances in one direction around the circle on the wrong side of the pieced pillow top.

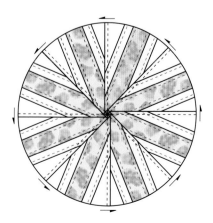

# Pillow Finishing

1. Layer the pieced fabric circle, right side up, on top of the 16" squares of batting and backing. Baste the layers together and quilt the pillow top as desired.

2. Position the remaining covered cording around the outer edge of the pillow top, joining the ends as directed on page 15. Baste in place a scant ½" from the raw edge.

3. Using the tissue pattern, cut the pillow back from the 15" square of light blue print.

4. With right sides together, pin the pillow back to the pieced and corded pillow top. Stitch ½" from the outer edge, leaving a 5" opening for turning.

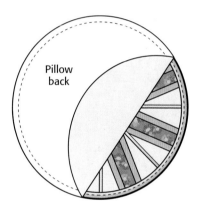

Pillow back

5. Turn the pillow cover right side out. Insert the pillow form. Slip-stitch the opening closed. Sew the decorative button in the center of the pillow.

Sew a button to the pillow center.

# Scrappy Flower Wedge Pillow

**Finished Size:** 14" diameter

*This pillow offers a fun way to use favorite fabric scraps. The piecing is easy, so why not make more than one and let your pillow garden grow?*

## Materials

*All yardages are based on 42"-wide fabric.*

⅞ yard total of assorted red fabric scraps for pieced wedges

¾ yard of green fabric for pillow back and covered cording

¼ yard total of assorted green fabric scraps for pieced wedges

16" x 16" square of scrap backing

16" x 16" square of batting

1½ yards of ¼"-diameter cotton cording for covered cording

14"-diameter knife-edge pillow form

15" x 15" square of tissue paper for pattern

2"-diameter decorative button for pillow center

## Cutting

*All measurements include ½"-wide seam allowances unless otherwise stated.*

**From the assorted red fabrics, cut:**
- An assortment of 8"-long strips in the following widths: 1½", 2½", and 3½"

**From the assorted green fabrics, cut:**
- 16 squares, 3" x 3"

**From the green fabric for pillow back, cut:**
- 2 strips, 2" x 42"
- 1 strip, 15" x 42"; crosscut 1 square, 15" x 15"

## Pillow-Top Assembly

1. Make a tissue-paper pattern for the wedge in an eight-wedge 14"-diameter pillow as directed on page 33.

2. Using ¼"-wide seam allowances, sew the red strips together to form scrappy rectangles that measure approximately 8" x 9". For a truly scrappy look, sew them together with haphazard seam widths. Make eight large pieced rectangles.

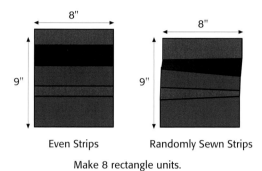

Even Strips    Randomly Sewn Strips
Make 8 rectangle units.

3. Cut a wedge from each scrappy rectangle.

Cut 8.

4. With right sides together, position a 3" green square across each outer point of each wedge. It's not necessary to position them exactly the same way at each edge. Stitch ¼" from the outer raw edge of each square. Trim the excess fabric even with the edge of the square. Flip the green pieces down and press toward the seam allowance. Use the wedge pattern piece to trim each piece to the original shape.

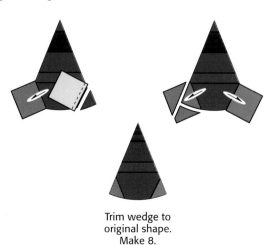

Trim wedge to original shape. Make 8.

5. Using ½"-wide seam allowances, sew the wedges together in pairs. Sew the resulting pairs together to complete the pillow top. Press all seam allowances in one direction around the circle on the wrong side of the pieced pillow top.

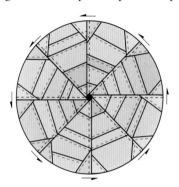

## Pillow Finishing

1. Layer the pieced fabric circle, right side up, on top of the 16" squares of batting and backing. Baste the layers together and quilt as desired.

2. Using ¼"-wide seams, sew the 2" x 42" green strips together and press the seam open. Use the strip to make covered cording as directed on page 14. Baste the cording in place along the outer edge of the pillow top, joining the ends as described on page 15.

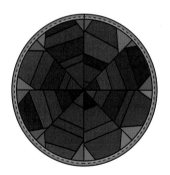

Baste cording in place.

3. Using the tissue pattern, cut the pillow back from the 15" green square.

4. With right sides together, pin the pillow back to the pieced and corded pillow top. Stitch ½" from the outer edge, leaving a 5" opening for turning.

5. Turn the pillow cover right side out. Insert the pillow form. Slip-stitch the opening closed. Sew the decorative button to the center of the pillow.

# Floral Wreath Pillow

**Finished Size:** 14" diameter

*Fussy cutting the wedges for this pillow top creates a wreath of flowers around the outer edge. Take time to shop for just the right floral print to make the "wreath." If florals don't match your decorating scheme, you can create similar results by fussy cutting the wedges from other prints.*

## Materials

*Yardage is based on 42"-wide fabric.*

1 yard of floral print for pillow back and covered cording, plus enough additional yardage to fussy cut 8 circle wedges of floral print fabric*

16" x 16" square of scrap backing

4" x 45" piece of scrap backing

16" x 16" square of batting

4" x 45" piece of batting

2½ yards of ⅛"-diameter cotton cording for covered cording

14"-diameter pillow form, 3" thick

15" x 15" square of tissue paper for pattern

1¼"-diameter decorative button for pillow center

* *Make the wedge pattern and take it with you when shopping to test the layout on the chosen fabric. See "Designer Tip" on page 41.*

## Cutting

*All measurements include ½"-wide seam allowances.*

**From the floral print, cut:**
- 1 strip, 15" x 42"; crosscut 1 square, 15" x 15"
- 2 strips, 4" x 42"
- 3 strips, 1½" x 42"

## Pillow-Top Assembly

1. Prepare a wedge-shaped pattern piece for a 14"-diameter pillow as directed on page 33.

2. Position the wedge pattern on the floral fabric (see "Designer Tip") and cut eight wedges with identical or similar placement of the floral motif at each outer curved edge. Take care to position the motif so that it won't be caught in the ½"-wide seam allowance at the outer curved edge.

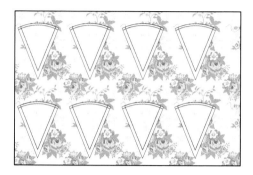

3. Using ½"-wide seam allowances, sew the wedges together in pairs. Sew the resulting pairs together to complete the pillow top. Press all seam allowances in one direction around the circle on the wrong side of the pieced pillow top.

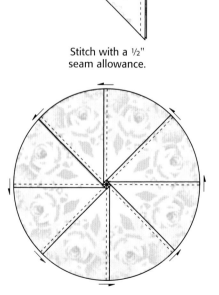

Stitch with a ½" seam allowance.

4. Layer the pieced fabric circle, right side up, on the 16" squares of batting and backing. Baste the layers together and quilt as desired.

5. Sew the 1½" x 42" floral-print strips together and press the seams open. Use the strip to cover the cotton cording as directed on page 14. Position the cording around the outer edge of the pieced pillow top and baste in place, joining the ends as directed on page 15. Set excess cording aside for the pillow back.

6. Using a ¼"-wide seam, sew the 4" x 42" floral-print strips together to make the boxing strip. Press the seam allowance open. Cut a 4" x 45" boxing strip from the longer strip.

7. Layer the strip on the 4" x 45" pieces of batting and backing and baste. Quilt as desired.

8. Using a ½"-wide seam allowance, sew the short ends of the quilted strip together. Trim the seam to ¼" and press open.

## Pillow Finishing

1. Using the pattern for a 14" finished round pillow, cut the pillow back from the 15" floral-print square.

2. Baste the remaining covered cording to the outer edge of the pillow back, joining the ends as you did for the pillow top.

3. Pin the boxing strip to the pieced and corded pillow top. Stitch ½" from the raw edges.

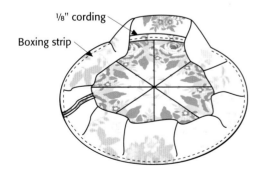

4. With right sides together, pin the boxing strip to the outer edge of the corded pillow back. Stitch, leaving a 5" opening for turning.

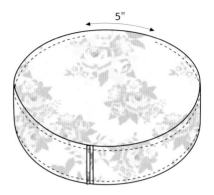

5. Turn the pillow cover right side out and insert the pillow form. Slip-stitch the opening closed. Sew the decorative button to the center of the pillow.

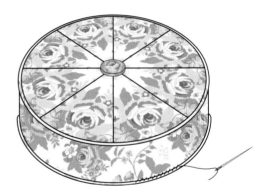

Slip-stitch opening closed.

# Leafy Heart Pillow

**Finished Length:** 16"

*A shirred boxing strip adds a lovely finish to this pretty pillow. Leaves and vine appliqués emphasize the pillow's curves. Use your favorite green fabric scraps in assorted prints and values to create the elegant appliquéd design.*

## Materials

*Yardage is based on 42"-wide fabric.*

1 yard of light green print for shirred boxing strip and pillow back

⅝ yard of off-white fabric for pillow top

¼ yard of dark green solid for bias vine

¼ yard total of assorted green print scraps for appliqué leaves

⅞ yard of scrap backing

18" x 18" square of batting

3 yards of ⅛"-diameter cotton cording for covered cording

16" box-edge heart-shaped pillow form

16" x 16" square of tissue paper

*Optional:* Small beads for embellishment

## Cutting

*All measurements include ½"-wide seam allowances unless otherwise stated.*

**From the off-white fabric, cut:**
- 1 square, 17" x 17"

**From the dark green solid, cut:**
- 4 bias strips, 1¼" wide, as directed for bias stems on page 10

**From the light green print, cut:**
- 1 square, 17" x 17"
- 3 strips, 3" x 42"
- 3 strips, 1½" x 42"

**From the scrap backing fabric, cut:**
- 1 square, 18" x 18"
- 2 strips, 3" x 42"

## Designer Tip

Use the leftover scraps of fabrics from the leaves to create a Crazy quilt design for the pillow back. Embellish with hand or machine embroidery to create a truly special pillow.

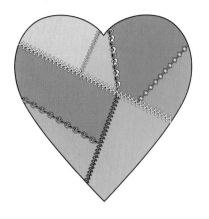

## Pillow-Top Assembly

1. Using the 16" square of tissue paper, draw a heart shape as shown on page 33. *This pattern does not have seam allowances added. You will add them later.* Center the pattern on the 17" square of white fabric and trace around the outer edge, using your favorite nonpermanent marking method.

2. Sew the dark green bias strips together to make a strip for the vine that is 36" long. Make bias vine as directed on page 10. The finished stem should be ⅜" wide.

3. Choose your favorite appliqué method: hand, machine, or fusible. Make a template for the leaves using the leaf pattern on page 46. If you will be turning under the edges of your appliqué shapes for hand appliqué, add a scant ¼"-wide turn-under allowance beyond the outer edges of the leaf shapes when you cut them from the assorted green fabrics. Cut the number of leaves indicated on the leaf pattern.

4. Using the illustration below as a guide and beginning at the bottom point, position the vine around the outer edge of the marked heart. Turn under the raw edges at the point to miter, tucking in any raw edges that protrude at the finished edges. Sew in place.

Leave at least 1" between
leaves and heart outline.

5. Position the leaves around the vine so that the outermost edge of any appliqué piece is roughly 1" from the outline. Sew or fuse the leaves in place.

6. Place the appliquéd pillow top, right side up, on the 18" squares of batting and backing. Baste the layers together and quilt as desired.

7. Machine baste ½" from the marked heart outline and cut away any excess fabric just outside the basting.

Baste ½" from outline.
Trim just outside basting.

8. Using a ¼"-wide seam, sew the 1½" x 42" light green strips together and press the seams open. Use the strip to cover the cotton cording as directed on page 14.

9. Beginning somewhere below the upper curved edge of the heart, position the cording along the outer edge of the heart shape. When you reach the lower point of the heart, clip the cording seam allowance so that you can work the cording smoothly into place. The resulting point on the pillow will really be a soft curve. Baste the covered cording in place, joining the cording ends as described on page 15. Set the remaining covered cording aside for the pillow back.

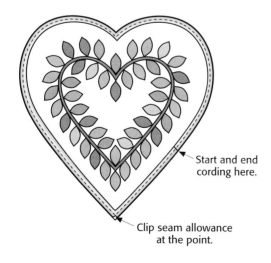

Start and end cording here.

Clip seam allowance at the point.

10. Embellish the pillow top with beads if desired.

## Pillow Finishing

1. Use the 16" tissue-paper heart to cut the pillow back from the 17" light green square, *adding a ½"-wide seam allowance all around when you cut it out.*

Cut heart, adding ½" seam allowance.

2. Baste the remaining cording to the outer edge of the pillow back, joining the ends as you did for the pillow front.

3. Using a ¼"-wide seam allowance, sew the 3" x 42" scrap backing strips together. Press the seam open. From the resulting strip, cut a 50"-long strip for the shirred boxing strip.

4. Using a ¼"-wide seam allowance, sew the 3" x 42" light green boxing strips together and press the seams open. Machine baste a scant ½" from each long raw edge of the strip.

5. Draw up the bobbin threads to gather both edges of the strip. Pin the gathered strip to the 3" x 50" backing strip, adjusting the gathers evenly. Stitch a scant ½" from the raw edges.

Draw up bobbin threads to shirr.

Baste boxing strip to backing strip.

6. Beginning at the lower point of the heart and 2" from the strip end, pin the gathered boxing strip to the completed pillow top. Stitch to the pillow top, joining the ends of the shirring strip at the point as shown. Trim away the excess boxing strip, leaving a ¼"-wide seam allowance. Press the seam open.

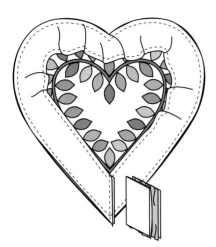

Stitch together at point. Trim excess.

7. Pin the pillow back to the remaining raw edge of the shirred boxing strip, making sure that the seam is at the point of the pillow back so that the top and bottom heart shapes are in the same position. Stitch, leaving a 6" opening for turning.

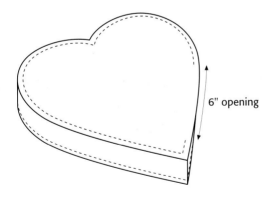

6" opening

8. Turn the pillow right side out and insert the pillow form. Slip-stitch the opening closed.

## Designer Tip

If you have a treasured antique or family quilt that has been damaged, salvage the "good" portions and use them to create keepsake pillow tops.

**Leaf**
Cut 44.

# Ruffled Heart Pillow

**Finished Length:** 16"

*An appliquéd border on this lovely pillow is the perfect "frame" for a photo transfer of a treasured family member—or a precious piece of needlework if you prefer.*

## Materials

*Yardage is based on 42"-wide fabric.*

⅞ yard of beige stripe for ruffle

⅝ yard of beige print for appliquéd border

8" x 10" photo transfer (or piece of needlework) for pillow center

18" x 18" square of scrap backing

18" x 18" square of batting

16" box-edge, heart-shaped pillow form

17" x 17" square of tissue paper for pattern

*Optional:* 1⅛ yards of decorative cording or trim to frame center

## Cutting

*All measurements include ½"-wide seam allowances unless otherwise stated.*

**From the beige print, cut:**
- 1 strip, 17" x 42"; crosscut 2 squares, 17" x 17"

**From the beige stripe, cut:**
- 3 strips, 8" x 42"

## Pillow-Top Assembly

1. Using the 17" square of tissue paper, draw a heart-shaped pattern as directed on page 33.

2. Layer the two 17" squares of beige print, with raw edges even, and pin the heart pattern in place. Cut out two hearts. Remove the pattern.

3. Center the photo transfer underneath the tissue-paper pattern and draw a heart shape to frame the

photo transfer as desired. Draw a second line ¼" inside the line for the frame to add a turn-under allowance.

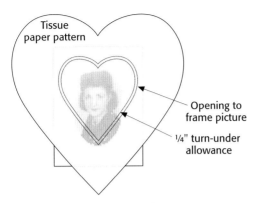

4. Position the marked pattern on top of one of the heart-shaped fabric pieces and cut out the center heart to make the heart-shaped opening. Position the "frame" over the photo transfer. Turn under ¼" around the inner edge of the frame, making ⅛"-long clips at the point and wherever necessary for a smoothly turned edge. Appliqué to the photo transfer. *Optional:* Position and pin the trim along the edge of the frame. Turn under the raw edges where the ends meet and stitch in place.

Cut out the opening to create a heart frame.

Appliqué heart frame to photo transfer.

5. Layer the appliquéd pillow top, right side up, on the 18" squares of batting and backing. Baste the layers together and quilt as desired.

6. Machine baste ⅛" from the raw edge of the heart pillow top, sewing through all layers. Trim the excess batting and backing even with the outer edge of the pillow top.

## Pillow Finishing

1. Using a ¼"-wide seam allowance, sew the 8" x 42" beige stripe strips together, end to end, to make a circle. Press the seams open.

2. Fold the ruffle in half with wrong sides together and raw edges even. Press. Machine baste ½" from the raw edges. Draw up the bobbin thread tails to gather the ruffle so it fits the outer edge of the pillow top. Pin in place and adjust the gathers evenly. Stitch in place.

3. With right sides together, stitch the remaining fabric heart to the ruffled pillow top. Leave a 5" opening for turning.

4. Turn the pillow right side out and insert the pillow form. Slip-stitch the opening closed.

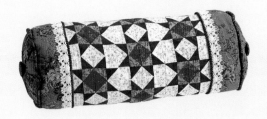

# Neckrolls

Traditionally, the tubular-shaped neckroll is used to support the space between your neck and shoulders. However, it is also a nice shape to use for visual variety with other decorative pillows on your bed or sofa.

To make a neckroll, you will construct a fabric cylinder with either flat, gathered, or pleated ends. The filler is either a purchased neckroll form or an insert made by rolling a sheet of polyester batting into the desired size as described.

To make your own insert, roll a sheet of polyester batting into a cylinder and whipstitch the outer edge of the batting to the layer beneath it. You can also make your own bolster by creating a muslin cover, following the directions for the plain bolster, and then stuffing it with polyester fiberfill to the desired firmness. Once stuffed, slip-stitch the opening closed to finish your custom-made insert.

Roll batting into bolster shape.
Whipstitch layers together.

# Garden Lattice Neckroll

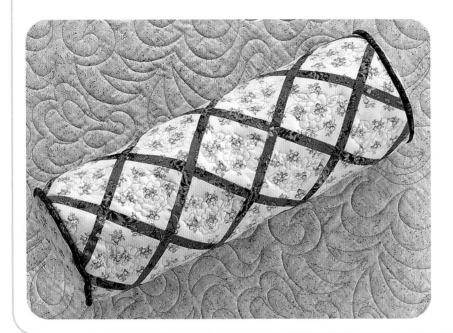

**Finished Size:** 6" x 18"

*A floral fabric crisscrossed with lattice sashing is easy to piece and makes a decorator pillow with a garden theme.*

## Materials

*Yardage is based on 42"-wide fabric.*

⅞ yard of pale green floral print for pillow cover

⅜ yard of medium green tone-on-tone print for lattice strips

¼ yard of dark green for covered cording

23" x 33" piece of scrap backing

23" x 33" piece of batting

1⅜ yards of ¼"-diameter cotton cording for covered cording

6" x 18" bolster form

Compass, tissue paper, and pencil

## Cutting

*All measurements include ¼"-wide seam allowances unless otherwise stated.*

**From the medium green tone-on-tone print, cut:**
- 7 strips, 1" x 42"; set 2 strips aside and crosscut the following pieces from the remaining 5 strips:
    - 8 sashing strips, 1" x 4"
    - 2 sashing strips, 1" x 10"
    - 2 sashing strips, 1" x 17"
    - 2 sashing strips, 1" x 24"
    - 1 sashing strip, 1" x 31"

**From the dark green fabric, cut:**
- 2 strips, 2" x 42"

**From the pale green floral print, cut:**
- 2 strips, 3½" x 42"
- 1 strip, 5½" x 42"; crosscut 4 squares, 5½" x 5½"; cut each square twice diagonally to make 16 setting triangles
- 1 rectangle, 9½" x 20"

**From the scrap backing, cut:**
- 1 square, 23" x 23"
- 1 strip, 10" x 22"

**From the batting, cut:**
- 1 square, 23" x 23"
- 1 strip, 10" x 22"

# Pillow-Cover Assembly

1. Sew a 1" x 42" medium green strip to the long edge of a 3½" x 42" pale green floral strip. Make a total of two identical strip sets. Press the seam allowance toward the medium green strip. Cut the strip sets into 3½"-wide sashed-block segments for a total of 24 segments.

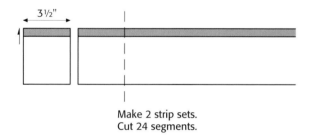

Make 2 strip sets.
Cut 24 segments.

2. With right sides together, sew a 1" x 4" sashing strip to a short edge of eight of the setting triangles. Make two sets of four that are mirror images of each other. Press the seam allowance toward the green sashing strip. Trim the excess even with the triangle edges.

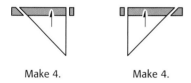

Make 4.          Make 4.

3. Arrange the sashed blocks, sashed and unsashed setting triangles, and the long sashing strips in diagonal rows as shown. Sew the pieces together in rows and press all seam allowances toward the sashing strips.

4. Sew the rows together with the long sashing strips between them. Press the seam allowances toward the sashing strips and trim the ends even with the setting-triangle edges.

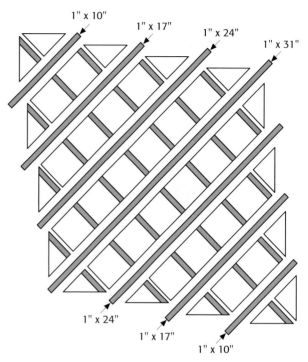

Sew rows and sashing strips together.

5. Layer the pillow cover with the 23" squares of batting and backing. Baste the layers together and quilt as desired. Fill the "windows" in the patchwork with the quilting design on page 52.

6. Machine baste a scant ¼" from the outer edge of the quilted pillow cover, stitching through all layers. Trim the excess batting and backing even with the pillow-cover edges.

7. Using a compass, draw a 7¼"-diameter circle on a piece of tissue paper and cut out. Trace around the pattern twice on the 9½" x 20" floral rectangle. Layer with the 10" x 22" pieces of batting and backing. Baste the layers together and quilt as desired.

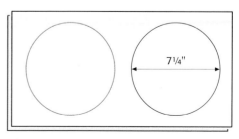

Trace two circles on green floral rectangle.
Quilt the layered fabric as desired.

8. Machine baste a scant ¼" from the outer edge of each circle. Cut each circle from the quilted layers.

## Pillow Finishing

1. Fold the pillow cover in half crosswise with right sides together and the 19"-long raw edges even. Beginning and ending 4" from each end, stitch ¼" from the long edges. Finger-press the seam open.

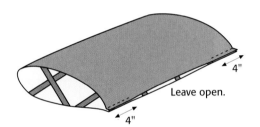

Begin and end stitching 4" from ends.

2. Following the directions on page 14 and using the 2" x 42" dark green strips, make two pieces of covered cording, each 22" long.

3. Turn the pillow cover right side out. Pin and sew the covered cording to the raw edges on the right side of the pillow cover. Use a ½"-wide seam allowance and join the cording ends as directed on page 15. *Turn the pillow cover wrong side out.*

Sew cording to each end of pillow cover.

4. With right sides together, pin an end circle to one end of the pillow cover. Clip into the pillow body as needed to ease it around the circle edge. (Clips should be no longer than ⅜".) Stitch ½" from the raw edges. Repeat at the other end.

5. Turn the pillow cover right side out through the opening and insert the pillow form. Slip-stitch the opening closed.

**Continuous-Line Quilting Design**
Start quilting at center.

# Stars All Around Neckroll

**Finished Size:** 6" x 18"

*A simple star block makes a big impact on this colorful neckroll.*

## Materials

*Yardage is based on 42"-wide fabric.*

¾ yard of light cream floral print for block background

⅝ yard of assorted dark red prints for star points

⅝ yard of medium dark red tone-on-tone print for star centers

⅝ yard of pink tone-on-tone print for star centers

⅝ yard of medium green tone-on-tone print for borders

¼ yard of dark green print for covered cording

23" x 33" piece of scrap backing

23" x 33" piece of batting

1⅜ yards of 1"- to 1½"-wide lace

1⅜ yards of red decorative trim

1⅜ yards of ¼"-diameter cotton cording for covered cording

6" x 18" bolster form

2 decorative or self-covered buttons, 1¼" diameter

*Optional:* Buttonhole twist or carpet thread for gathered end treatment

## Cutting

*All measurements include ¼"-wide seam allowances unless otherwise stated.*

**From the assorted dark red prints, cut:**
- 1 rectangle, 15" x 25"

**From the medium dark red tone-on-tone print, cut:**
- 1 square, 15" x 15"

**From the pink tone-on-tone print, cut:**
- 1 strip, 15" x 42"; crosscut 1 square, 15" x 15"

**From the light cream floral print, cut:**
- 3 strips, 1½" x 42"; crosscut 60 squares, 1½" x 1½"
- 1 strip, 15" x 42"; crosscut 1 rectangle, 15" x 25"

**From the medium green tone-on-tone print, cut:**
- 2 strips, 3¾" x 42"; crosscut 2 strips, 3¾" x 20½"
- 2 strips, 4½" x 42"; crosscut 2 strips, 4½" x 20½"

**From the dark green print, cut:**
- 2 strips, 2" x 42"; crosscut 2 strips, 2" x 23"

**From the scrap backing, cut:**
- 1 square, 23" x 23"
- 1 strip, 10" x 22"

**From the batting, cut:**
- 1 square, 23" x 23"
- 1 strip, 10" x 22"

## Star Block Assembly

1. Following the directions on pages 10–11 and using the dark red print and light cream floral 15" x 25" rectangles, make half-square-triangle units. Cut the bias strips 2" wide. Press the seams toward the dark red strips in each strip unit. Cut 120 half-square-triangle units, 2" x 2", from the strip units and trim to 1½" x 1½".

Make 120.

Make 60.

2. Use the medium dark red tone-on-tone and pink tone-on-tone 15" squares to make 60 half-square-triangle units.

3. Arrange the 1½" light cream squares and the half-square-triangle units from steps 1 and 2 as shown below to make a total of 13 star blocks and four half-star blocks. Sew the units together in rows and press the seams in opposite directions from row to row. Sew the rows together to make each of 13 star blocks and four half-star units. Press the seams in one direction.

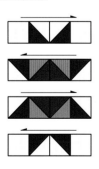
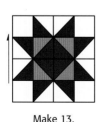

Make 13.

Make 4.

## Pillow-Cover Assembly

1. Arrange the star blocks and half-star units in three vertical rows, beginning and ending the first and third rows with the half-star units. Sew the blocks together in vertical rows and press the seams in opposite directions from row to row. Sew the rows together and press the seams in one direction.

2. Cut two 22" lengths each of red decorative trim and lace. Using a ½"-wide seam allowance, baste the lace and trim to one raw edge of each of the medium green strips.

3. With right sides together, sew a 3¾" x 20½" medium green strip to each long edge of the patchwork. Press the seams toward the patchwork.

4. Layer the pillow top with the 23" squares of batting and backing. Baste the layers together and quilt as desired.

5. Machine baste a scant ¼" from the outer edge of the pillow cover through all layers. Trim the excess batting and backing even with the pillow top.

6. Fold the pillow cover in half crosswise with right sides together and the 19"-long raw edges even. Stitch ¼" from the edges and finger-press the seam open.

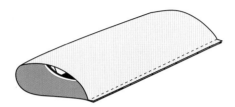

7. Turn the pillow cover right side out. Cut two lengths of ¼"-diameter cording, each 22" long. Wrap a 2"-wide green strip around each piece of cord to make covered cording as directed on page 14. Using a ½"-wide seam allowance, sew the cording to the raw edges of each end of the pillow cover, joining the ends of the cording as directed on page 15.

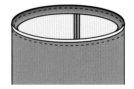

Sew covered cording to each end.

8. For the pillow ends, fold each 4½" x 20½" medium green strip in half crosswise with right sides together and short raw edges even. Stitch ¼" from the raw edges.

9. Turn under and press ½" at one raw edge on each end piece and topstitch ¼" from the folded edge.

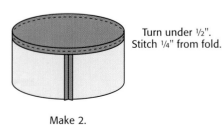

Turn under ½". Stitch ¼" from fold.

Make 2.

# Pillow Finishing

1. With right sides together, raw edges even, and seam lines matching, pin one medium green end piece to the pillow cover. Stitch ½" from the long edges. Repeat with the remaining end piece.

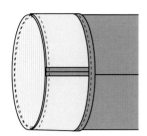

Stitch end piece to pillow cover.

2. Insert the bolster form.

3. To complete the ends, choose one of the following two finishing options:

   *For gathered ends,* use a hand-sewing needle and strong thread (buttonhole twist or carpet thread) to make running stitches along the finished edge of each end piece. Pull up the stitches to gather and draw the ends into the center. Tie off the thread securely.

   *For pleated ends,* make evenly spaced, overlapping pleats to draw the excess fullness into the center at each end of the pillow. Hand sew the layers together to secure. Sew a large covered or purchased button in the center at each end of the finished neckroll.

Pleat or gather end pieces.

# Ruffled Drawstring Neckroll

**Finished Size:** 6" x 18"

*This sweetly feminine, ruffled neckroll invites you to cuddle up with a good book.*

## Materials

*Yardage is based on 42"-wide fabric.*

1⅛ yards of light purple tone-on-tone print for pillow cover and ruffles

⅜ yard of purple plaid for pillow-cover center

⅛ yard of dark purple print for covered cording

22" x 23" piece of scrap backing

22" x 23" piece of batting

1⅜ yards of 3"- to 3¼"-wide lace trim

1⅜ yards of ⅛"-diameter cotton cording for covered cording

1⅜ yards of ribbon or decorative cord for drawstring

6" x 18" bolster form

## Cutting

*All measurements include ½"-wide seam allowances.*

**From the dark purple print, cut:**

- 1 strip, 1½" x 42"; crosscut 2 strips, 1½" x 21"

**From the lace trim, cut:**

- 2 pieces, 21" long

**From the purple plaid, cut:**

- 1 strip, 9" x 21"

**From the light purple tone-on-tone print, cut:**

- 1 strip, 6½" x 42"; crosscut 2 strips, 6½" x 21"
- 3 strips, 7" x 42"; from 1 of the strips, crosscut 2 strips, 7" x 21"
- 1 strip, 4½" x 42"; crosscut 2 strips, 4½" x 21"

# Pillow-Cover Assembly

1. Cut the cotton cording into two pieces, each 21" long. Using the 1½" x 21" dark purple strips, make covered cording as directed on page 14.

2. Baste a piece of cording to each long edge of the 9" x 21" purple plaid strip. Baste a piece of lace to the right side on one long edge of each 6½" x 21" light purple strip.

Baste cording and lace to strips.

3. With right sides together, sew a light purple/lace strip to each long edge of the corded plaid strip. Press the seam toward the plaid center.

4. Layer the pillow cover with the 22" x 23" pieces of batting and backing. Baste the layers together and quilt as desired. Trim the excess backing and batting even with the outer edges of the pillow cover.

5. Fold the quilted pillow cover in half with right sides together and stitch ½" from the raw edges.

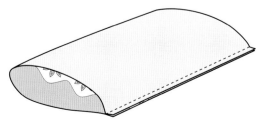

Stitch with a ½" seam.

6. Fold each 4½" x 21" light purple strip in half crosswise with raw edges even. Stitch ½" from the raw edges, stopping 2" from one end. Press the seam open.

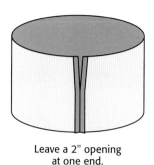

Leave a 2" opening at one end.

7. To form a casing on each end piece from step 6, turn under and press ¼" at the seam end with the unstitched section. Turn under and press an additional ½". Edgestitch close to the inner folded edge.

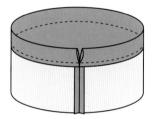

Edgestitch to make casing.

8. For each ruffle, sew a 7" x 42" light purple strip to a 7" x 21" light purple strip, using a ¼"-wide seam allowance. Press the seam open.

9. With right sides together and using a ¼"-wide seam allowance, sew the short ends of each ruffle strip together to make a circle. Press the seam open.

10. Fold each ruffle circle in half lengthwise with wrong sides together and raw edges even. Press. Machine baste a scant ½" from the raw edges.

11. Pull on the bobbin threads to gather a ruffle so it fits one end of the pillow cover. Pin in place, adjusting the gathers evenly. Baste in place. Repeat with the remaining ruffle.

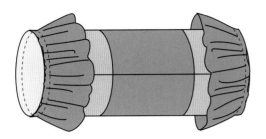

## Pillow Finishing

1. With right sides together, seam lines matching, and raw edges even, pin an end section to each end on top of the ruffle. Stitch ½" from the raw edges at each end of the pillow cover.

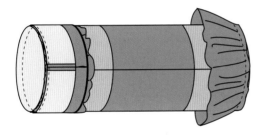

2. Thread ribbon or cord through the casing at each end.

3. Insert the bolster form; draw up the ribbon or cord and tie in a bow.

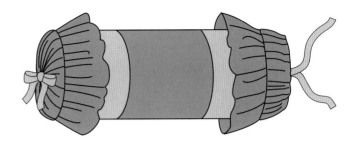

## Designer Tip

The open space on this pillow cover could become the background for an autographed keepsake pillow. Cut the center panel from a light-colored solid or tone-on-tone print and provide a permanent-ink, Micron pen for the autographs. This would make the perfect keepsake for a baby shower, a get-well gift, or even a Sweet Sixteen slumber party.

# Pillow Shams and Pillowcases

*Pillow shams are attractive, loose-fitting pillow covers that usually coordinate with the bed covering. As a decorative hideaway for bed pillows, shams usually have a simple closure, making it easy to slip them on and off for cleaning. Directions for whole-cloth trapunto, pieced, and appliquéd shams are included in this section. The bonus project is a lovely pillowcase.*

*When designing your own sham or pillowcase projects, you will need to know the dimensions for the size of bed pillow you are using.*

Standard: *20" x 26"*
Queen: *20" x 30"*
European: *26" x 26"*

# Whole-Cloth Trapunto Pillow Shams

**Finished Size:** 20" x 30" (queen size)

*The simple tie closures on this pillow sham make it an easy and elegant covering for a bed pillow. See "Designer Tip" on page 62 for other decorative options.*

## Materials for Two Shams

*Yardage is based on 42"-wide fabric.*

3⅝ yards of off-white tone-on-tone print or solid for sham

2 pieces of high-loft polyester batting, 25" x 35", for trapunto

4 pieces of scrap backing, 25" x 35"

2 pieces of batting, 25" x 35"

Water-soluble basting thread

## Cutting for Two Shams

*All measurements include ½"-wide seam allowances.*

**From the off-white tone-on-tone, cut:**

- 4 strips, 24" x 42"; crosscut 4 rectangles, 24" x 34"
- 2 strips, 4" x 42"; crosscut 2 strips, 4" x 41"
- 6 strips, 2½" x 42"; crosscut 12 strips, 2½" x 21"

# Sham Assembly

*(Instructions for One Sham)*

1. Use your favorite nonpermanent marking method to draw a 16" x 24" rectangle in the center of a 24" x 34" piece of off-white fabric. Enlarge the pattern on page 63 as directed. Referring to the illustration below, trace the trapunto design inside the marked 16" x 24" space.

2. Place the marked pillow front, right side up, on a 25" x 35" piece of high-loft batting. Pin in place.

3. Follow the directions for machine trapunto beginning on page 12 to complete the pillow top.

4. After completing the trapunto and additional quilting outside the raised motifs, add rows of channel quilting in the area outside the quilted rectangle. Space the rows 1" apart. The finished quilted area should measure 20" x 30". Trim the layers to measure 21" x 31", which allows for a ½"-wide seam allowance to each side of the rectangle. Machine baste ⅛" from the raw edges, stitching through all layers.

Close meandering quilting in areas surrounding trapunto

5. Layer a 24" x 34" off-white rectangle with a 25" x 35" piece of batting and a 25" x 35" piece of backing. Baste the layers together and channel quilt, spacing the rows 1" apart. Trim the pillow back to measure 21" x 31". Machine baste ⅛" from the raw edges, stitching through all layers.

6. With right sides together and long edges even, fold each 2½" x 21" off-white strip in half lengthwise for the ties. Stitch ¼" from the raw edges. Turn each strip right side out and press. At one end of each tube, turn ½" to the inside and press. Stitch through all layers to finish the end.

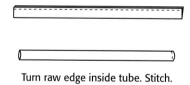

Turn raw edge inside tube. Stitch.

# Sham Finishing

1. With right sides together and raw edges even, pin the sham front to the sham back along three edges, leaving one short edge open. Stitch ½" from the three pinned edges. Turn the sham right side out.

2. Pin a tie to the sham front, centering it along the opening edge. Pin two more ties to the sham front, spacing them 5" apart. Pin three ties to the sham back in the same manner. Machine baste the ties in place, stitching a scant ½" from the sham raw edge.

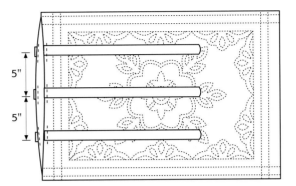

Baste ties to sham front and back.

3. For the sham facing, fold a 4" x 41" off-white strip in half with right sides together and short ends even to form a circle. Stitch ½" from the raw edges. Press the seam open. Turn under and press ½" on one raw edge of the fabric circle.

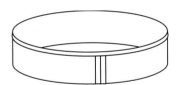

Turn under and press ½".

4. With right sides together, pin the sham facing to the sham over the ties. Stitch ½" from the raw edges. Turn the facing to the inside of the sham and press. Slip-stitch the inner edge of the facing to the inside layer of the pillow sham.

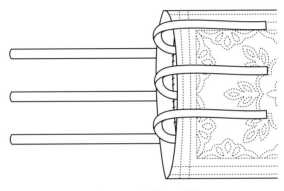

Turn facing to inside of pillow and slip-stitch the edge.

## Designer Tip

Consider these decorative options to replace the tie closures on the sham:

- A row of buttonholes on the sham front and buttons sewn in place on the inside of the sham back at the opening edge
- A row of matching buttonholes on the sham front and the sham back with tassels looped through them
- A row of buttonholes on the sham front and back with sets of buttons joined with cording

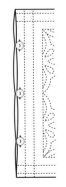

Single Buttons and Buttonholes

Tassels through Buttonholes

Double Buttons and Buttonholes

Flip pattern along this line.

**Whole-Cloth Trapunto Pillow Sham**
Enlarge pattern 170%.

# Blueberry Vine Pillow Shams

**Finished Size:** 20" x 26"

(standard size)

*Appliquéd blueberries and a trailing vine create a traditional look for this standard-sized pillow sham. Flange borders and an envelope closure in the back make the sham construction fast and easy.*

## Materials for Two Shams

*Yardage is based on 42"-wide fabric.*

3 yards of dark green tone-on-tone print for flange and sham back

¾ yard of tan tone-on-tone print for sham front

½ yard of dark green fabric for appliquéd bias vine

⅞ yard total of assorted green scraps for appliquéd leaves

⅜ yard total of assorted blue scraps for appliquéd berries

2 pieces of scrap backing, 22" x 28"

2 pieces of batting, 22" x 28"

## Cutting for Two Shams

*All measurements include ½"-wide seam allowances. Use the templates on page 65.*

**From the ½ yard of dark green fabric, cut:**
- 8 bias strips, 1¼" wide, for the vines as directed on page 10 to make 180" total

**From the tan tone-on-tone print, cut:**
- 1 strip, 22" x 42"; crosscut 2 rectangles, 16" x 22"

**From the dark green tone-on-tone print, cut:**
- 12 strips, 3½" x 42"; crosscut:
    - 4 strips, 3½" x 16"
    - 4 strips, 3½" x 27"
    - 4 strips, 3½" x 21"
    - 4 strips, 3½" x 33"
- 2 strips, 26" x 42"; crosscut 4 rectangles, 21" x 26"

## Sham Assembly

*(Instructions for One Sham)*

1. Choose your favorite appliqué method: hand, machine, or fusible. Using the patterns on page 65, make templates for the berries and leaves. If you will be turning under the edges of your appliqué shapes, add a scant ¼" allowance beyond the outer edge of each appliqué shape as you cut it from the appropriate fabric. From the assorted green scraps, cut 80 leaves for each sham (160 for two). From the assorted blue scraps, cut 58 berries for each sham (116 for two).

2. Using ¼"-wide seam allowances, sew the dark green bias strips together to make a strip that is 180" long. Referring to the directions on page 10, prepare the vine. It should measure ⅜" wide when finished.

3. Using the illustration below as a guide, position the vine, leaves, and berries on the 16" x 22" tan rectangle. Make sure that the outermost appliqués are at least ¾" from the edge.

4. Sew the 3½" x 16" dark green border strips to the short edges of the appliquéd rectangle. Press the seam allowances toward the borders. Sew the 3½" x 27" dark green strips to the top and bottom edges. Press the seam allowances toward the borders.

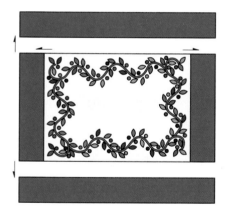

5. Layer the appliquéd rectangle with a 22" x 28" piece of batting and a 22" x 28" piece of backing. Baste the layers together and quilt as desired. Stitch ⅛" from the outer edges of the appliquéd rectangle through all layers. Trim the batting and backing even with the rectangle edges.

6. Sew the 3½" x 21" dark green flange strips to the short edges of the pillow front. Press the seam allowances toward the flanges. Sew the 3½" x 33" dark green flange strips to the top and bottom edges. Press the seam allowances toward the flanges.

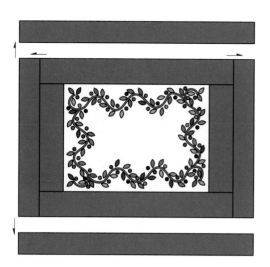

## Sham Finishing

1. Sew a 1" double-fold hem on one 21" edge of each 21" x 26" dark green rectangle for the sham back as directed on page 16.

2. With right sides together and raw edges even, position one of the hemmed pieces on the pillow front. Add the remaining hemmed piece and pin the layers together. Stitch ½" from the raw edges.

3. Turn the sham right side out. Press the outer edges. With the pillow sham face up, stitch along the seam line through all layers to create the flange.

4. Insert a bed pillow in the completed sham.

Stitch in the ditch of the seam line to create flange.

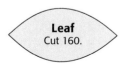

# Whole-Cloth Rose Medallion Trapunto Pillow Shams

**Finished Size:** 27" x 37"
(fits queen-size bed pillows)

*These elegant pillow shams feature trapunto roses, surrounded by straight-line quilting, and a scalloped flange around the edges.*

## Materials for Two Shams

*Yardage is based on 42"-wide fabric.*

5 yards of red print for pillow sham front and back

2 pieces of high-loft batting, 10" x 13", for rose medallion trapunto

2 pieces of scrap backing, 22" x 32"

2 pieces of batting, 22" x 32"

*Optional:* 3½ yards of ¼"-diameter cording for outlining trapunto medallion

Water-soluble basting thread

Bodkin

Tissue paper for scallop pattern

## Cutting for Two Shams

*All measurements include ½"-wide seam allowances.*

**From the red print, cut:**

- 1 strip, 31" x 42"; crosscut 2 pieces, 21" x 31"
- 8 strips, 4½" x 42"; crosscut:
  4 flange strips, 4½" x 29"
  4 flange strips, 4½" x 39"
- 4 pieces, 24" x 42"; crosscut 4 pieces, 24" x 28"

## Sham Assembly

*(Instructions for One Sham)*

1. Use your favorite nonpermanent marking method to trace the roses and leaves on page 70 in the center of the 21" x 31" pillow front. Enlarge the design on page 70 as directed. Mark diagonal quilting lines,

spaced ¾" apart inside the oval frame and 1½" apart outside the oval frame.

*Optional:* To create a raised frame around the rose motif, draw another line ½" from the first oval during this step.

2. With right side up, center the marked sham on top of a 10" x 13" piece of high-loft batting, making sure the batting is positioned behind all of the rose motif. Pin in place.

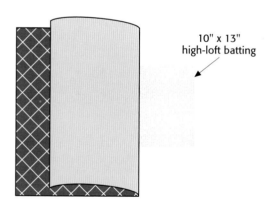

10" x 13" high-loft batting

3. With water-soluble basting thread in the needle and regular thread in your bobbin, stitch just inside (¹⁄₁₆") the outline of the roses and leaves.

4. On the wrong side, trim away the batting that is not behind the raised trapunto design. Use blunt scissors to trim as close as possible, being careful not to cut the sham front.

Cut away excess batting.

5. Layer the 21" x 31" pillow front fabric with a 22" x 32" rectangle of batting and a 22" x 32" rectangle of backing. Baste the layers together and quilt on the marked lines (including the second oval if you are making a raised oval frame around the central rose motif).

*Optional:* To create the raised frame, make a small slit through the backing and batting between the two stitching lines for the frame. Use a bodkin to pull the ¼"-diameter cording between the quilted layers in the frame. Pull the bodkin out of the slit and trim the cord ends even. Tuck the ends inside and whipstitch the opening closed.

6. Stitch ⅛" from the raw edges of the sham front through all layers. Trim the excess batting and backing even with the sham front edges.

7. With right sides together, center and pin a 4½" x 39" flange strip at the upper edge of the sham front. Stitch, beginning and ending the stitching ½" from the sham-front raw edges. Press the seam allowance toward the flange. Repeat at the opposite edge. Add the 4½" x 29" flange strips to the short edges of the sham in the same manner.

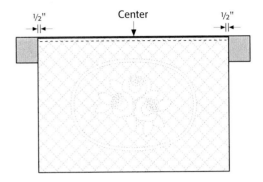

8. With the sham front, right side up, on a flat surface, turn under one of the flange ends at a 45° angle to make a mitered corner. Pin in place and check the corner to make sure it is square by placing a square transparent ruler on top. Adjust the folded edge if necessary. Press the fold and slip-stitch by hand. On the wrong side, trim the excess flange fabric, leaving a ⅜"-wide seam allowance to press open. Repeat at the remaining three corners.

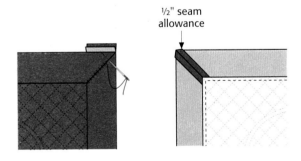

9. Cut two tissue-paper strips, 3½" x 20", and two strips, 3½" x 37". To mark the scalloped edge, use the curved shapes on page 69. Trace the curves for the sides and corners onto each piece of paper. Adjust the pattern as needed to create gentle curves and use a marking pen to draw smooth connecting curves on the tracing paper. Pin the pattern sections to the flanges and tape the sections together

if desired. Cut the scallops, following the curved lines on the tissue strips.

## Sham Finishing

1. Sew a 1" double-fold hem on one 24" edge of each 24" x 28" piece for the sham back as directed on page 16.

2. With right sides together and raw edges even, position one of the hemmed pieces on the pillow front. Add the remaining hemmed piece and pin the layers together. Stitch ½" from the scalloped edges. Remove the pins and trim the excess fabric even with the raw edges of the scallops. Clip the curves and turn the pillow sham right side out. Press the outer edges.

3. With the pillow sham face up, stitch along the seam line through all layers to create the flange.

4. Insert a bed pillow in the completed sham.

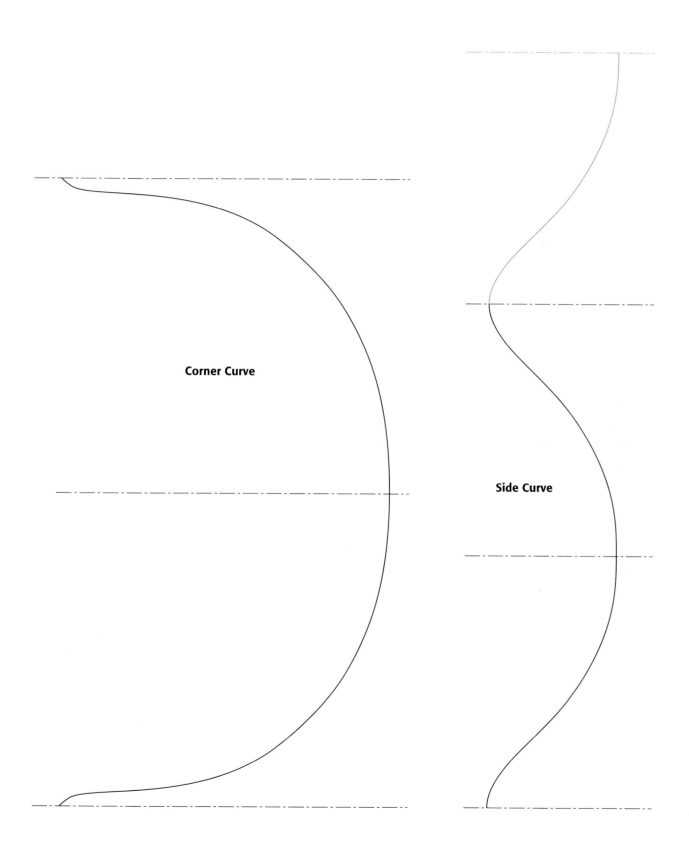

**Corner Curve**

**Side Curve**

This outer line is optional. See "Optional" in step 1 on pages 66–67.

**Whole-Cloth Rose Medallion Pattern**
Enlarge pattern 200%.

# Appliquéd Rose Pillow Shams

**Finished Size:** 27" x 33"
(fits standard-size bed pillows)

*Large, old-fashioned roses provide an attractive focal point in the center of these thoroughly feminine pillow shams.*

## Designer Tip

Instead of cutting and appliquéing multilayer roses, cut large roses from a floral print and fuse them in place for the old-fashioned look of broderie perse appliqué.

## Materials for Two Shams

*Yardage is based on 42"-wide fabric.*

4 yards of large-scale floral print for sham ruffles and back

⅞ yard of medium-scale floral print for sham front

⅝ yard of cream tone-on-tone print for medallion background

½ yard of green tone-on-tone print for trim around medallion

¼ yard of assorted reds in medium to dark tones for rose appliqués

¼ yard of assorted greens for leaf appliqués

3½ yards of ¼"-wide red flat trim for outlining oval

2 pieces of scrap backing, 22" x 28"

2 pieces of batting, 22" x 28"

14½" x 19½" piece of tissue paper for pattern

## Cutting for Two Shams

*All measurements include ½"-wide seam allowances unless otherwise stated.*

**From the cream tone-on-tone print, cut:**
- 1 strip, 15" x 42"; crosscut 2 rectangles, 15" x 20"

**From the medium-scale floral print, cut:**
- 1 strip, 27" x 42"; crosscut 2 rectangles, 21" x 27"

**From the green tone-on-tone print, cut:**
- 6 strips, 1¾" x 42"

**From the large-scale floral print, cut:**
- 12 ruffle strips, 8" x 42"
- 2 strips, 18" x 42"; crosscut 4 rectangles, 18" x 21"

# Sham Assembly

*(Instructions for One Sham)*

1. To make a pattern for the oval medallion, fold the 14½" x 19½" piece of tissue paper in half and then in half again. Draw a gentle curve from one folded edge to the other and cut along the line. Open the pattern piece.

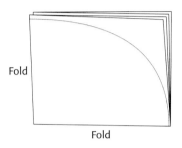

Fold

Fold

2. Pin the pattern to a 15" x 20" cream rectangle and cut out the oval.

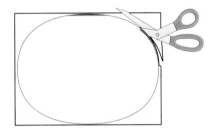

3. Turn under ¼" at the outer edge of the oval and stitch in place by hand or machine. Center the oval on a 21" x 27" rectangle of the medium-scale floral print.

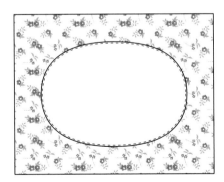

Turn edges under ¼" and sew the oval
to the medium-scale floral rectangle.

4. On the wrong side, trim away the floral print fabric ¼" inside the stitching line, taking care not to cut the fabric layer beneath it.

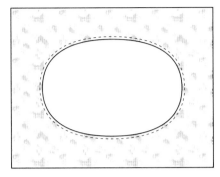

On the wrong side, trim center oval ¼" from stitching.

5. Choose your favorite appliqué method: hand, machine, or fusible. Using the patterns on page 74, make templates for the roses and leaves. If you will be turning under the edges of your appliqué shapes, add a scant ¼" allowance beyond the outer edge of each appliqué shape as you cut it from the appropriate fabric. Cut the required number of rose and leaf pieces from the red and green fabrics as indicated on the pattern.

6. Following the illustration below as a guide, position the roses and leaves in the center of the oval. Sew or fuse in place.

7. Layer the appliquéd sham front with a 22" x 28" rectangle of batting and a 22" x 28" rectangle of backing. Baste the layers together and quilt as desired. Machine stitch ⅛" for the outer raw edge of the sham front. Trim the excess batting and backing even with the sham front raw edges.

8. Using ¼"-wide seams, stitch the 1¾"-wide green strips together end to end to make one long strip. Cut a 108"-long piece from the strip. Sew the short ends together to make a circle. Press all seams open.

9. Turn under and press ¼" at each edge of the continuous strip and stitch in place with a decorative machine stitch. Machine baste ½" from one of the finished edges.

Turn under long edges ¼".
Secure with decorative stitch.
Baste ½" from one edge.

10. Pull on the bobbin threads to gather the ruffle so it fits around the medallion edge. Pin in place, adjusting the gathers evenly all around. Sew in place and stitch decorative trim in place on top to cover the stitching.

11. Using ¼"-wide seam allowances, sew six 8"-wide large-scale floral strips together to make one long piece for the ruffle. Sew the remaining ends together to make a large circle of fabric. Press all seams open.

12. Fold the ruffle strip in half with wrong sides together and raw edges even. Press. Machine baste a scant ½" from the raw edge. Pull the bobbin thread to gather the ruffle. Distributing the gathers evenly, pin the ruffle to the outer edge of the sham front with raw edges even. Machine baste in place a scant ½" from the raw edges.

Machine baste ruffle to sham front.

## Sham Finishing

1. Sew a 1" double-fold hem on one 21" edge of two 18" x 21" large-scale floral rectangles for the sham back as directed on page 16.

2. With right sides together and raw edges even, position one of the hemmed pieces on the sham front over the ruffle. Add the remaining hemmed piece and pin the layers together. Stitch ½" from the raw edges.

3. Turn the sham right side out and insert a bed pillow.

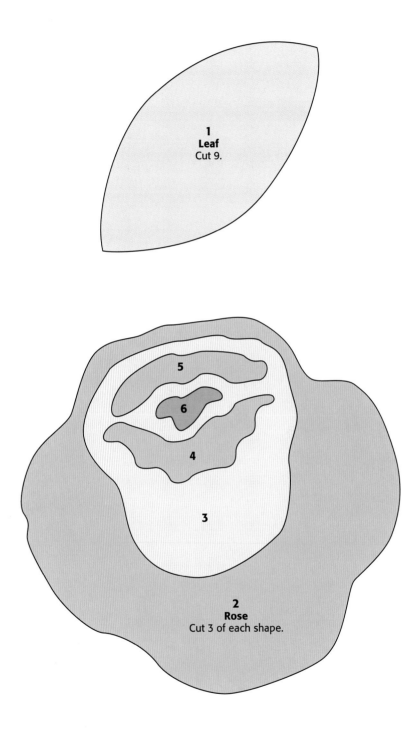

**1**
**Leaf**
Cut 9.

**2**
**Rose**
Cut 3 of each shape.

5

6

4

3

# Pieced European Pillow Shams

**Finished Size:** 26" x 26"
(without ruffle)

*Combine a simple pieced
pattern, a pleated ruffle, and
pearl-button embellishments,
and you have a set of
elegant oversized pillow shams.*

## Materials for Two Shams

*Yardage is based on 42"-wide fabric.*

4¼ yards of light green for ruffles and sham back

1 yard of white solid or tone-on-tone print for
  patchwork

¾ yard of light green solid for patchwork

¾ yard of light green print for patchwork

½ yard of beige stripe for covered cording

2 pieces of scrap backing, 28" x 28"

2 pieces of batting, 28" x 28"

6½ yards of ¼"-diameter cotton cording for covered
  cording

84 decorative buttons, ½" diameter

## Cutting for Two Shams

*All measurements for the patchwork include ¼"-wide
seam allowances. Measurements for the pillow assembly
include ½"-wide seam allowances.*

**From the light green solid, cut:**
- 7 strips, 3½" x 42"

**From the light green print, cut:**
- 7 strips, 3½" x 42"

**From the white fabric, cut:**
- 11 strips, 2½" x 42"; crosscut 168 squares,
  2½" x 2½"

**From the beige stripe, cut:**
- 6 strips, 2" x 42"

**From the light green ruffle fabric, cut:**
- 16 strips, 5" x 42"
- 2 strips, 27" x 42"; crosscut 4 pieces, 18" x 27"

# Sham Assembly

*(Instructions for One Sham)*

1. Arrange the 3½"-wide light green print and solid strips in pairs with right sides together. Cut a total of 85 sets of squares from the strip sets. Follow the directions in method one on page 10 to make half-square-triangle units, each 2½" x 2½" square. You should have 85 units for each pillow sham (170 total for two shams).

2. Arrange seven light green half-square-triangle units and six white 2½" squares in alternating fashion and sew together. Press the seams in one direction. Repeat to make a total of seven identical strips.

Make 7.

3. Arrange seven white 2½" squares and six light green half-square-triangle units in alternating fashion and sew together. Press the seams in one direction (opposite from the pressing direction in step 2). Repeat to make a total of six identical strips.

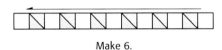

Make 6.

4. Arrange the pieced strips from steps 2 and 3 in alternating fashion and sew the rows together. Press the seams in one direction.

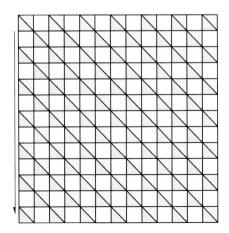

Sew rows together.

5. Layer the pieced sham front with a 28" square of batting and a 28" square of backing. Baste the layers together and quilt as desired. Stitch ⅛" from the raw edges of the patchwork, sewing through all layers. Trim the excess batting and backing even with the edges of the patchwork.

6. Using ¼"-wide seams, sew the 2"-wide beige stripe strips together to create a continuous fabric strip. Using the strip and the ¼"-diameter cording, make covered cording as directed on pages 14–15.

7. Position and baste the cording to the outer edge of the sham front. Note that the cording seam allowance will extend ¼" beyond the raw edge of the sham front around the outside edge of the pieced pillow top. Join the ends of the cording as directed on page 15.

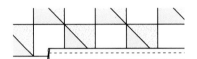

Cording seam allowance extends
¼" beyond sham edge.

8. Sew eight 5"-wide light green ruffle strips together to create one continuous length. Fold the strip in half with wrong sides together and press. To make the 2"-wide box pleats, fold the fabric onto itself and then back again.

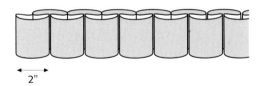

2"

9. Pin the ruffle to the pieced sham front, aligning the raw edges with the raw edge of the covered cording. Each pleat fold should match a seam line in the pieced sham front.

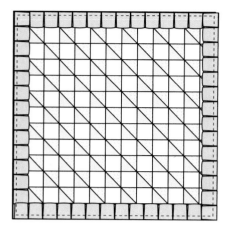

10. Sew the ends of the ruffle together so that the seam is invisible from the front, positioning it in a fold if possible.

11. Stitch the ruffle in place a scant ½" from the raw edges.

## Sham Finishing

1. Sew a 1" double-fold hem on one 27" edge of two 18" x 27" light green pieces for the sham back as directed on page 16.

2. With right sides together and raw edges even, position one of the hemmed pieces on the sham front. Add the remaining hemmed piece and pin the layers together. Stitch ½" from the raw edges.

3. Turn the sham right side out and sew a button in the center of each white square. Insert a European-size (26" x 26") pillow into the finished sham.

## Designer Tip

Instead of pearl embellishments in the squares, use your embroidery machine to add embroidered motifs. To do this, complete the patchwork pillow top and back it with a lightweight cutaway stabilizer. Then embroider the motifs in the desired squares. You may leave the stabilizer in place or cut it close to the outer edges of each embroidered motif.

Another decorative option for this pillow top is to fussy cut the plain squares from a floral print so that the motifs are centered in each square.

Fussy-cut a floral print to use in place of the white solid fabric.

# Decorative Pillowcases

**Finished Size:**
20" x 31" (standard)
and 20" x 35" (queen)

*Imagine the fun you'll have
selecting just the right fabric
and trims for your own
custom-made pillowcases
to coordinate with your quilts
and other bedding.*

## Materials for Two Pillowcases

*Yardage is based on 42"-wide fabric.*

|  | Pillow Size | |
|---|---|---|
|  | **Standard** | **Queen** |
| Fabric for pillowcase panel | 1⅝ yards | 2 yards |
| Fabric for contrasting band | ⅞ yard | ⅞ yard |
| Fabric for flat piping trim | ¼ yard | ¼ yard |
| Decorative trim (optional) | 2⅝ yards | 2⅝ yards |

## Cutting for Two Pillowcases

*All measurements include ½"-wide seam allowances.*

|  |  | Pillow Size | |
|---|---|---|---|
|  |  | **Standard** | **Queen** |
| *Fabric* | *No. of Strips* | *Strip Size* | |
| Flat piping | 2 | 1½" x 42" | 1½" x 42" |
| Contrasting band | 2 | 13" x 41" | 13" x 41" |
| Pillowcase panel | 2 | 26" x 41" | 30" x 41" |

## Pillowcase Assembly

*(Instructions for One Pillowcase)*

1. Fold the flat piping strip in half with wrong sides together and raw edges even. Press.

2. Pin the folded strip (and a 43"-long piece of decorative trim if desired) to one long edge of a 13" x 41" contrasting band. Machine baste a scant ½" from the raw edges.

3. With right sides together, pin the piped edge of the band to one long edge of a pillowcase panel. Stitch ½" from the raw edges. Press the seam toward the band.

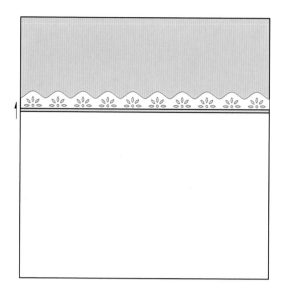

4. Fold the pillowcase in half lengthwise with right sides together and raw edges even. Beginning at the folded edge, stitch ½" from the raw edges, pivoting at the corner and continuing to the band edge. Turn under and press ½" at the raw edge of the band.

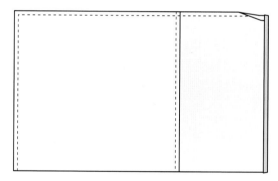

Turn under ½" at edge.

5. Turn the band to the inside of the pillowcase with the folded edge just past the stitching line. Press. Baste in place.

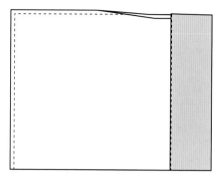

Baste folded edge of band in place at seam line.

6. Turn the pillowcase right side out. Topstitch or edgestitch along the band seam line through all layers to catch the folded inner edge of the band. Remove the basting.

Topstitch or edgestitch through all layers.

# Bibliography

Pahl, Ellen, ed. *The Quilters Ultimate Visual Guide.* Emmaus, Penn.: Rodale Press, 1997.

Simplicity Pattern Company, Inc. *Simplicity's Simply the Best Home Decorating Book.* New York: Simon & Schuster, 1993.

Sunset Books. *Simply Pillows.* Menlo Park, Calif.: Sunset Books, Inc., 1998.

Walner, Hari. *Exploring Machine Trapunto: New Dimensions.* Lafayette, Calif.: C & T Publishing, Inc., 1999.

# About the Author

Pamela Lindquist is a self-taught seamstress with more than 30 years of sewing experience, including sewing quilts as gifts for family and friends. Needlework and sewing have been an important form of personal expression and relaxation for Pam since she was a child. School, career, and family kept her busy and away from serious quilting projects for a while, but her interest was rekindled when her 25-year-old sewing machine, a high school graduation gift, needed to be replaced. While shopping for a machine, Pam discovered new quilt designs, construction techniques, and tools that inspired her to take up quilting again in earnest. She is the author of another home-decorating book published by Martingale & Company, *Sweet Dreams.* Pam lives in Eugene, Oregon, with her husband and two teenage children.